▼

Basic
Weight
Training

Thomas D. Fahey

California State University, Chico

▼

Mayfield Publishing Company
Mountain View
California

▼

To
My Father, the Old Carioca

Library of Congress Cataloging-in-Publication Data
Fahey, Thomas D. (Thomas Davin)
    Basic weight training.

    Bibliography: p.
    Includes index.
    1. Weight training.   I. Title.
GV546.F25 1989   613.7'1   88-13910
ISBN 0-87484-875-X

Manufactured in the United States of America
    10 9 8 7 6 5

Mayfield Publishing Company
1240 Villa Street
Mountain View, California 94041

Sponsoring editor, James Bull; production editor, Linda Toy; manuscript editor,
Anthony Steenkamp; text and cover designer, Andrew Ogus; cover photographer,
© 1988 Claudia Kunin for EXCEL, The Exercise Company; illustrator, Raychel
Ciemma. The text was set in 10/12 Memphis by Alphatype and printed on
50# Finch Opaque by George Banta Company.

Contents

► **CHAPTER SEVEN**

Exercises for the Lower Body   105

► **CHAPTER EIGHT**

Nutrition for Weight-Trainers   122

▶ **APPENDIX ONE**

Muscular System   147

▶ **APPENDIX TWO**

Sample Weight Programs to Build Strength for Sports   149

Preface

Weight training has become a world-wide obsession—from Ipanema to Iowa, people are lifting weights in the hope of developing firm, healthy-looking bodies. Athletes have become increasingly sophisticated in the use of resistive exercise and proper nutrition for improving sports performance. Unfortunately, their programs are often too complicated and cumbersome for the average person. *Basic Weight Training* was written to provide a primer for this enjoyable and beneficial activity. I've tried to furnish all the necessary information while including a minimal amount of scientific jargon.

Organization

Chapters 1 and 2 present the basic principles of weight training—the scientific basis of the activity. I've tried to translate the latest information from the sports medicine literature in a manner that will be clear to undergraduates. Chapters 3 through 7 describe the various major exercises that make up almost all weight programs. Chapter 8 presents important information from sports nutritionists on ergogenic aids and weight control, separating fact from fiction in this very controversial area. Appendix One illustrates the muscular system. Appendix Two presents programs tailored specifically for a number of selected activities.

Features

Basic Weight Training has many features that make it unique among weight training books. It contains the latest information from the medical, exercise physiology, and sports medicine literature, presented in a manner that is simple and easy to understand. Topics include anabolic steroids, amino acids, other ergogenic aids, basic muscle physiology, weight control, and body building secrets for toning up. Every exercise is described in detail and accompanied by a figure clearly showing the major muscles it develops. Safety is stressed throughout. Caution statements are included whenever a point is particularly important for preventing injury or avoiding an accident. The appendixes include detailed anatomical charts and suggested programs for a variety of activities. The back cover includes a workout card, so students can track their progress during the course.

Acknowledgements

Any book is the product of more than the person who wrote it. I'm indebted to the people at Mayfield Publishing, including Jim Bull, Linda Toy, Andrew Ogus, and Raychel Ciemma for their efforts in editing and producing this book. I'm grateful for the many valuable suggestions made by reviewers of the manuscript: Victor Buccola, California Polytechnic State University, San Luis Obispo; Bill Kutzer, California State University, Sacramento; Richard Streid, California State University, Northridge; and John Ramsey, California State University, Northridge. I'm particularly indebted to the many athletes and coaches who taught me the art of weight training, including Art Burns, John Powell, Bob Lualhati, Carl Wallen, Lachsen Akka, Richard Marks, Dave MacKenzie, Steve Hendersen, and Tom Carey.

▼

CHAPTER ONE

Weight Training and Your Fitness Program

Pumping iron has become extremely popular throughout the world. Although athletes such as football players, discus throwers, and wrestlers have included weight training in their fitness programs for many years, only recently have large numbers of non-athletes trained with weights. Now, gyms are crowded with people of all ages who are pushing weights in an attempt to look better, feel better, and perform to their potential. These people realize that a few hours of training each week will give them stronger, firmer bodies and increased strength that will carry over into other activities. People who train with weights can handle their body weight better in activities such as skiing and rock climbing, hitting the ball harder in tennis or racketball, and running faster in volleyball or softball. Have you ever wondered how all those hard bodies on the beach got that way? They paid their dues in the weight room. Now is the time for you to begin reaping all of the benefits that weight training can provide.

There are many ways to begin a weight training program. You can take a class, join a gym, or buy a set of weights for your home. Weight training has joined the high tech age. Some weight machines can adjust the resistance to your ability and keep track of your progress. Other machines can adjust to your body size and provide a variable load as you perform the exercise. However, you don't need fancy weight machines to receive the beneficial effects of weight training. For every major muscle group in your body, there are exercises that require only simple equipment.

Is motivation a problem? Do you have problems staying with a program? Today, it is easier than ever to start and stay on a program that will provide you with the long-term benefits of weight training. Take a class at school, at the local gym, at the "Y," or at a sports medicine center. A class provides you with a place and time to train as well as someone to teach you the basic exercises and principles of weight training. Taking a class helps motivate you to train consistently. Because you have made a basic commitment to attend the class, you are more likely to devote the time needed to meet your goal.

Are you the solitary type? You can set up a home gym that can either substitute for a program at the local gym or supplement your weight training class. People interested in home fitness products will find an array of relatively inexpensive, high quality products available that can provide many of the benefits of a well-equipped gym. In short, there is a way to fit weight training into almost anyone's fitness program.

THE BENEFITS OF WEIGHT TRAINING

Weight training provides many advantages that other forms of physical training do not. The benefits include a more muscular body, increased strength and power, improved sports performance, enhanced self-image, and a competitive outlet. It is an activity in which almost all people can achieve rapid gains and improve themselves. This can be said of almost no other sport or form of exercise. For example, you might take tennis lessons for years without being able to consistently hit the ball over the net. After a year of weight training, however, you are almost guaranteed stronger muscles and a well-shaped body.

A weight training program, by itself, is not enough to develop and maintain optimal health and fitness. Most people should also participate in a well-rounded health promotion program that includes endurance (aerobic exercise), strength, and flexibility exercises as well as proper nutrition and good health habits. Endurance exercise is necessary to strengthen the heart, lungs, and circulatory system and to help prevent coronary artery disease. Flexibility training helps maintain normal joint movement, which may prevent injury and disability (particularly as you grow older). Proper nutrition is necessary for providing energy and nutrients for a healthy body and for preventing diseases such as cancer and coronary heart disease. A healthy lifestyle also involves not smoking, handling emotional stress properly, having good personal hygiene, and maintaining a good body composition (acceptable body fat per lean body mass). In addition, weight training is an important part in the overall program of developing a healthy, successful, and invigorating way of life.

Weight Training and Your Body

Weight training will give your muscles that tight athletic look that many people wish to achieve. For women, weight training provides shapely, firm muscles that cannot be obtained by dieting or from most other forms of exercise. Because women have low levels of male hormones, they do not readily develop large muscles from weight training. Rather, they tend to lose weight and inches, slim down, and develop strength, all of which carries over into other activities. Men, on the other hand, do increase muscle size from weight training. No other training activity can provide the large arms, big chest, rippled abdominal muscles, and powerful legs that weight training can. If you want to look good on the beach, you had better spend some time in the weight room!

Weight training will not do it all, however. A shapely body requires that you watch what you eat and that you expend plenty of calories in endurance exercise. In addition, it wouldn't hurt to have genetics on your side. Some people are naturally fatter or thinner than the "ideal." Weight training, endurance exercise, and proper diet will measurably improve your body and your health but cannot change your basic body structure, which is inherited.

Increased Strength and Power

Increased strength and power is an advantage in daily life and can positively affect your health. The ability to exert force is an advantage in tasks ranging from shoveling snow to lifting suitcases at the airport. Everyday activities such as unscrewing tops of jars, pushing cars, and lifting heavy children are much easier if you are strong.

Strength training also makes muscles, tendons, and ligaments stronger and less susceptible to injury. This increased strength of the musculoskeletal system, while of obvious benefit in sport, may protect against injury and disability related to everyday activities. For example, back pain affects over eighty percent of the American public, and studies have shown that people with higher levels of muscle strength are much less susceptible to back pain.

Improved Sports Performance

Have you ever skied, hiked, or played tennis with someone who has poor muscle strength? They tire more easily and are less effective in the activity. People with stronger muscles, given the same level of skill, can hit tennis balls and baseballs harder, get over the edge of a ski better, and jump higher. Most athletes have known for years that weight training improves performance. In sports requiring strength and speed, such as football, discus throwing, and shot put, weight training is a cornerstone of the conditioning program. Weight training has completely changed the complexion of these sports. For example, in the National Football League during the 1950s, it was not unusual to see 200-pound linemen. Now, 275-pound linemen are common. Athletes have become this big through years of weight training.

Weight training is also an advantage in endurance sports such as distance running and swimming. In these sports, great emphasis is placed on cardiovascular capacity. Success in endurance sports is also determined by the ability to achieve and maintain a fast running or swimming speed, which requires muscle strength. This strength can be developed through weight training.

Whether you are an athlete or just a person who likes to exercise and play sports, increased strength can make you better in the physical activities that you enjoy. Staying in shape through sports is a lot more fun than doing boring exercise routines for the sake of health. Weight training, when practiced along with sports skills, enhances your enjoyment of sports by making you more successful and capable of handling more advanced techniques.

Enhanced Self-Image

Few activities have as positive an effect on self-image as weight training. This activity provides benefits that everyone can see, and in a relatively short time. People who develop attractive, fit, and healthy-looking bodies naturally feel good about themselves. Weight training helps many people to radiate self-confidence and is a good form of personal therapy.

Competitive Outlet

Weight training can also provide a competitive outlet. Some people use weight training to become more competitive in sports they enjoy. For others, such as body-builders and weight-lifters, lifting weights is central to the competition. Anyone can achieve satisfaction from the competitive aspects of weight training. When you lift weights, you are competing against yourself for PR's (Personal Records). You are always trying to achieve one more pull-up, a few more pounds on your bench press, or an inch more on your biceps. **There is no more meaningful competition than that which you have against yourself.**

HOW WEIGHT TRAINING AFFECTS YOUR BODY

Weight training has a number of beneficial effects on your body including increased muscle size, improved strength of muscles, tendons, and ligaments, enhanced coordination between the nervous and muscular systems, and increased tissue structural support.

Muscle Structure and Strength

Muscles move the skeleton. They are attached to bones by tendons. When a muscle contracts, it shortens and pulls on the tendon, causing the bone to move. Strong muscles make it much easier to move the skeleton. In addition, strong tendons are less prone to injury.

Muscles are made up of individual muscle cells—called muscle fibers—connected in bundles. Muscle fibers are composed of subunits called myofibrils (Figure 1–1). The myofibrils are divided into units called myofilaments (actin and myosin), which slide across each other to cause muscle contraction (Figure 1–2). One of the goals of our weight training program is to increase the size of muscle fibers by increasing the number of myofibrils. This process of making larger muscle fibers is called **hypertrophy**. In general, larger muscles tend to be stronger.

Figure 1–1 *Components of skeletal muscle tissue: fasciculi, muscle fiber, myofibrils, and myofilaments.*

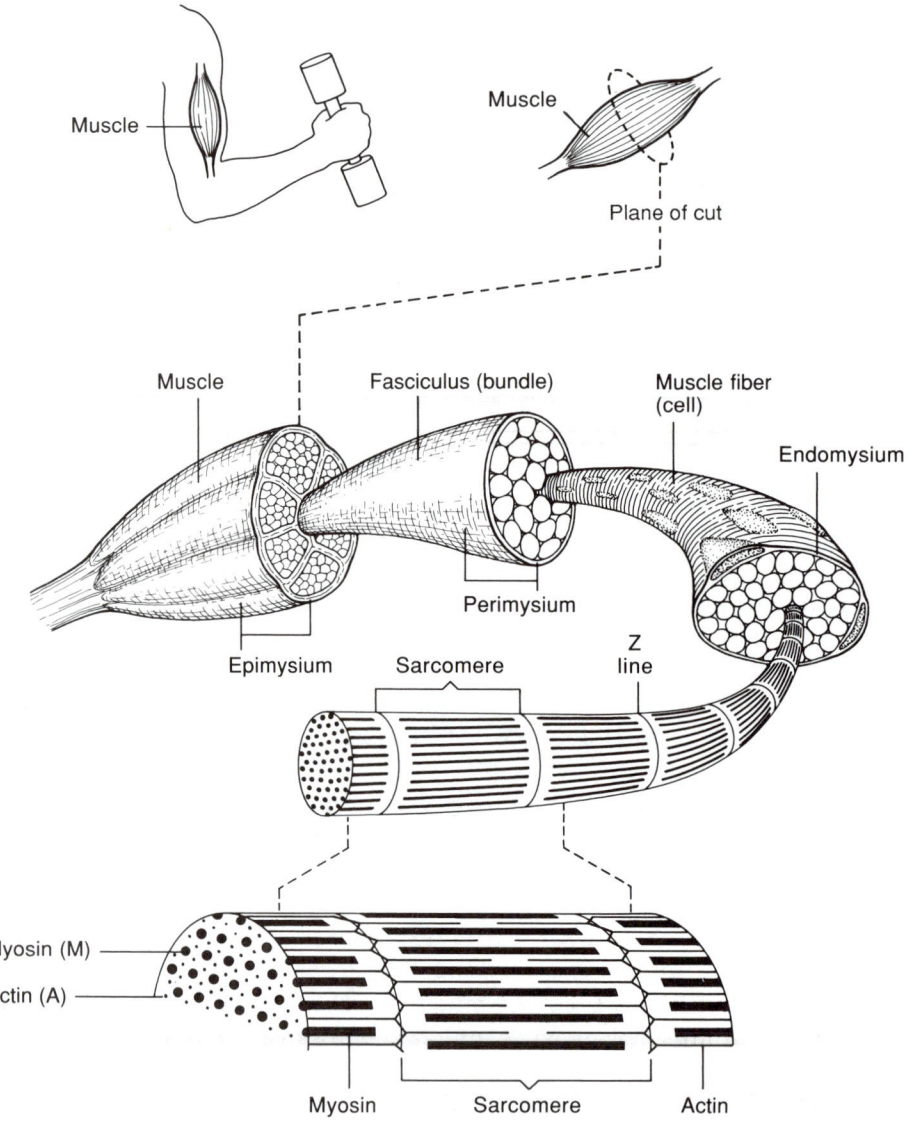

Figure 1–2 *The sliding filament theory of muscle contraction. The myosin filaments pull on the actin filaments causing the muscle fiber to shorten. The basic contractile unit of the muscle fiber is the sarcomere. The Z membrane serves as the outer boundary of the sarcomere.*

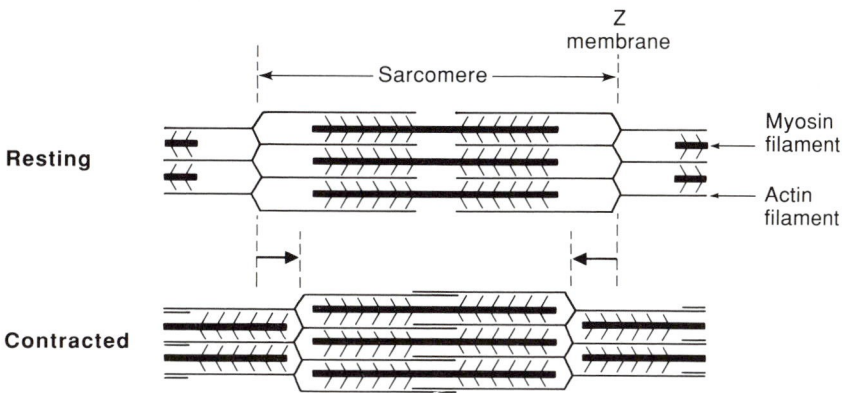

Do muscle fibers become larger with training or do they increase in number? This question has been debated for over eighty years. The bulk of evidence suggests that strength training causes muscle fibers to become larger (hypertrophy) rather than increase in number (hyperplasia). However, some evidence suggests that muscle fibers can increase in number under certain circumstances or that some exceptionally strong people may be born with more muscle fibers than others. But, muscle hypertrophy has been accepted as the most important way of making muscles stronger.

The Motor Unit Muscle fibers receive the signal to contract from nerves connected to the spinal column. Nerve-muscle combinations are called motor units (Figure 1–3). A motor nerve (a nerve connected to muscle fibers) may be connected to as few as one muscle fiber to more than 150 muscle fibers. Powerful muscles, such as the quadriceps in the upper leg, have large motor units—each motor nerve is connected to many muscle fibers. Smaller muscles, such as those found around the eye, have much smaller motor units.

There are three types of motor units: fast glycolytic (FG), fast oxidative glycolytic (FOG), and slow oxidative (SO), which are subdivided according to their ability to contract and their resistance to fatigue. The type of motor

Figure 1–3 *The motor unit. The motor unit is composed of a motor nerve and a number of muscle fibers.*

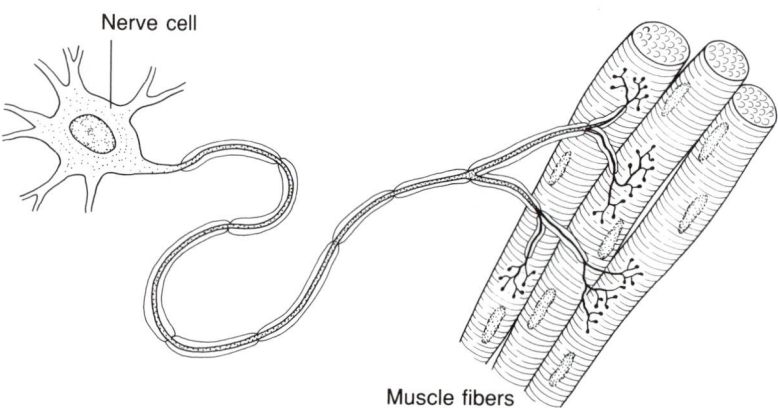

units used in any muscle depends upon the requirements of the muscle contraction. The body selects FG fibers to control the muscles used for lifting heavy weights or sprinting because those muscles are fast and powerful. However, SO fibers are selected to control prolonged standing or slow walking because those muscles are more resistant to fatigue.

The body exerts force by calling upon one or more motor units to contract. This process of calling upon motor units to contract is called **motor unit recruitment**. When a motor unit calls upon its fibers to contract, all of the fibers contract to their maximum capacity. When you want to pick up a small weight, for example, you use relatively few motor units to accomplish the task. However, when you want to pick up a large weight, you will use many motor units. Training with weights improves the ability to recruit (call upon) motor units to exert force.

Increased Strength Through Improved Motor Unit Recruitment Motor "learning" is a very important way of increasing strength. Weight training improves your nervous system's ability to coordinate the recruitment of muscle fibers. Through this process, the body can increase its strength even if muscle size fails to increase. Improved recruitment is the most effective means of improving strength in older people.

In summary, weight training increases muscle strength in two basic ways. First, you increase the size of your muscle fibers, and second, you improve the ability to call upon motor units to exert force. The first process involves muscle hypertrophy, which means making muscles larger. The second process involves improved motor unit recruitment, which means calling upon motor units to exert force.

Ligaments and Tendons

Tendons connect muscle to bone, and ligaments connect bones to other bones. Both of these tissues have little or no blood supply, so they have a very low metabolism (energy consumption level). Consequently, they heal slowly when injured. Scientists have discovered that these structures can be strengthened through exercise. This is fortunate because when you develop stronger muscles through weight training, you become capable of running faster, lifting more weight, and jumping higher. All of these activities place more stress on the joints of the body. If you have trained with weights, your joints will be capable of tolerating the increased loads encountered in vigorous physical activity.

TRAINING AND ADAPTATION

The human body is a remarkable organism because it adapts its function to the physical requirements of daily life. If you are required to lift heavy objects regularly, then your muscles grow stronger. On the other hand, if you seldom do any exercise, then your muscles will be small, reflecting your sedentary lifestyle.

Stress Adaptation

When your body is subjected to stress, it either adapts or breaks down. When the stress is excessive, tissues become injured. The purpose of a training program is to subject the body to reasonable physical stress but not subject it to such severe stress that it cannot adapt. In other words, your training program should cause you to become stronger without injury. Every time you walk into the weight room, you should ask yourself this question: "How is this workout helping my body to adapt and become stronger?" Sometimes you will have to train harder to ensure the optimal rate of adaptation. At other times, such as when you have trained excessively and are fatigued, you will need to rest in order to get the most from your program. The following list defines some terms the weight training student should become familiar with.

Overload, the basis of stress adaptation, subjects the body to more stress than it is accustomed to. The components of overload are load, repetition, rest, and frequency. Each factor affects the other. For example, if load is high, then repetitions are usually lower and rest is longer.

Load is the intensity of exercise and, in weight training, refers to the amount of resistance or weight used during an exercise. In general, the greater the load, the greater the fatigue and required recovery time. Of all the components of overload, load is probably the most important for increasing strength. A recommended load for beginners is a weight that can be lifted 10 times during a particular exercise.

Repetition refers to the number of times an exercise is performed during a set. A set is a group of repetitions followed by rest. More favorable adaptation tends to occur when the load is administered more than once. In weight training, particularly among beginners, 5–12 repetitions and 2–4 sets per exercise are usual.

Rest is the amount of time between sets. Rest is vitally important for adaptation and should be applied according to the nature of the desired outcome. For example, a weight lifter who desires maximum strength is most concerned with load and as a result requires a considerable amount of rest between exercises. A runner, on the other hand, is more concerned with muscular endurance (the ability to sustain prolonged exercise), so he or she will use shorter rest intervals between sets. Beginners should rest approximately one to two minutes between exercises.

Frequency refers to the number of training sessions per week. Most people who train with weights do so three times per week, but frequency may vary between two to five times per week. Frequency of training must be determined according to the desired outcome. While severe training programs have improved performance in many sports, such workouts must be tempered with proper recovery periods or injury may result. More is not always better. Excessive training programs can also lead to overtraining, which will stall progress or result in injury.

Specificity of Training

The body adapts specifically to the stress of exercise. The adaptation to endurance exercise (for example, distance running or swimming) is different from the adaptation to strength exercise and power exercise (for example, weight training and sprinting). Likewise, arm or shoulder exercises will do very little to strengthen the legs. Any training program should reflect the desired adaptation: the more the training exercises match the requirements of the sport, the more valuable will be the outcome.

The exercises you choose for your weight training program must also reflect the desired outcome. If you are weight training to get in shape for skiing, then concentrate on lower body exercises. You should also work on your upper body but not to the same degree. If you are interested in improving your appearance, then perform more varied exercises, concentrating on the larger muscles and those parts of the body that need work. Your body will adapt to the stresses that you subject it to, so your program must be carefully structured in order to achieve the desired outcome.

Individual Differences

We were not all created equal when it comes to physical skills, strength, and endurance. Differences between individuals determine the ability to perform physical skills and respond to an exercise program. These differences are based on the intensity of the training program and genetics, both of which are vital to performance. A naturally talented person will seldom be successful if he or she does not devote sufficient time to training. Alternatively, a person without that innate talent may find it difficult to perform at a superior level, even if subjected to the most arduous training regimen.

Training can help you overcome your weaknesses. Even the weakest among us can achieve a respectable level of strength and muscle mass if the training program is intense enough. But, you cannot expect to see miraculous changes overnight. If you are patient and train consistently and intelligently, you will receive the desired results.

Reversibility

Among coaches and exercise leaders there is an old saying that "if you don't use it, you lose it." The purpose of weight training, or any other kind of conditioning exercise, is to stress the body more than it is accustomed to. When muscles are subjected to an increased load, they respond by growing larger and becoming stronger. On the other hand, if less than normal stress is placed on the muscles, as occurs when a limb is put in a plaster cast, then the muscles shrink (atrophy).

It is important that you stay reasonably fit year-round. It is much easier to maintain a level of fitness than it is to regain a level of fitness that was lost through deconditioning. High levels of fitness require many years of training and involve small stages of progression. A person who is physically fit got that way through a series of small gains. The body cannot be forced to adapt rapidly; an attempt to do so will only cause injury.

Effects of Sex and Age

The concentration of male hormones, such as testosterone, has a large influence on the muscles' response to weight training. Thus men and women respond differently to weight training, as do younger and older men because of the dissimilarities in hormone systems. Women have very low concentrations of these hormones, so they experience very little muscle growth in response to strength exercises. Instead, women tend to get stronger by improving the efficiency of their nervous systems to call upon motor units to contract their muscle fibers. However, they do achieve some increase in muscle size, particularly if the training program is intense and practiced for an extended period. Likewise, older men increase strength more through improved neuromuscular coordination rather than through muscle enlargement.

Scientific Training Principles

When you train, you are acting very much like a doctor who works to cure a disease. You administer a treatment (a workout involving exercise such as weight training, swimming, or running) in an effort to alter the body's functioning. When you participate in a weight training program, you are stimulating your body to manufacture more muscle protein so that your muscles will get larger and stronger. You are compelling your body to adapt and improve its function.

The goal of a training program should be to increase fitness and prevent injury (Figure 1–4). Every time you plan a workout, you should ask

Figure 1–4 *Stress adaptation. Some exercise stress causes improved fitness, but excessive stress causes injury.*

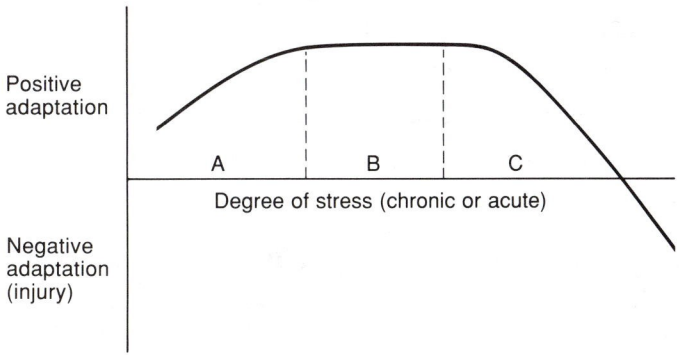

yourself the question: "Is this exercise session going to help my body improve its functioning?" The answer will not always be yes. Sometimes rest is more appropriate than exercise, or a less intense workout is occasionally better than an exhausting one.

Adhering to the following eleven principles of training is the best way of achieving the objectives of your weight training program. These principles detail instructions for developing optimal physical fitness and will result in improved performance with a minimum risk of injury. In addition, they are a guide to gradual and long-lasting fitness development. While the specifics of these training principles differ in various sports, the essence of the principles is the same for all.

1. **Train specifically for your sport or primary physical interests.** If you are primarily concerned with general fitness, choose a well-rounded program that concentrates on the major muscle groups. In addition to your weight training routine, your program should include endurance and flexibility exercises. If you are a body builder, work on your weaknesses, even if the exercises necessary to correct them are unpleasant. Among football players, lower body power is much more important than achieving a 400-lb bench press. Analyze what you are doing. A well designed program that considers the principle of specificity of training will be more effective and less time-consuming.

Table 1–1 The Principles of Training
▶ Train specifically for your sport
▶ Train all year round
▶ Get in shape gradually
▶ Listen to your body
▶ Train first for volume (more repetitions) and only later for intensity (heavier weights)
▶ Cycle the volume and intensity of your workouts
▶ Don't overtrain
▶ Train systematically
▶ Train your mind
▶ Become a student of your sport
▶ Keep your exercise program in its proper perspective

2. **Train all year round.** People lose a tremendous amount of physical fitness through deconditioning. They become much more susceptible to injury if they try to get back in shape rapidly. Set up a year-round program; have specific goals and procedures for each period of the year; and stick to them. Have alternative training plans for when the weather is bad or when you don't have access to a weight room. For example, if you are on a trip, substitute calisthenic exercises—such as push-ups and knee bends—for your regular routine. Set aside a certain portion of the day for your exercise routine to ensure you will get that workout. Your exercise time is the part of the day that belongs to you; don't let anyone take it away.

3. **Get in shape gradually.** Give your body time to adapt to the stress of exercise. Overzealous training leads to injury and overtraining. Numerous recent studies have shown that muscle is more susceptible to injury during the early phases of conditioning. Training is a stress that the body must overcome. Intense conditioning when you are not prepared for it will lead to injury and delay progress. Staying in fairly good shape all year long is much easier than

trying to achieve fitness in a few months. When the big push comes, such as when you are buffing it up for the beach or trying to fit into your new dress or suit for the high school reunion, it's much easier to apply a little pressure rather than attempting to go for a crash conditioning program.

4. **Listen to your body.** While the expression is a bit weathered, it is true nonetheless. Do not stick to your planned program too stubbornly if it doesn't feel right. Sometimes your body needs rest more than it needs exercise. Most studies show that the *absolute* intensity is perhaps the chief factor in improving fitness. Typically an overtrained person has not recovered enough to train at the optimal intensity; consequently, a few days rest is sometimes necessary to provide enough recovery to again allow for more intense training. On the other hand, don't train by whim. It is essential to try to maintain a structured workout program.

5. **Train first for volume (reps) and only later for intensity (heavy loads).** Soft tissues require a great deal of time to adjust to the rigors of training. For example, studies show that ligaments and tendons adjust very slowly to the stresses of exercise. First, prepare your body for heavy training by performing more repetitions during the workout to avoid injury. During later training sessions, when the body is better conditioned, more weight and fewer repetitions can be employed to increase strength at a faster rate.

6. **Cycle (vary) the volume and intensity of your workouts.** This technique, sometimes called periodization of training, allows the body to recover more fully and to train hard when hard training is called for. While sophisticated workout cycles are most relevant to athletes, individuals interested in general fitness can also benefit from the principle of cycled training. The principle is simple: it involves performing a particular exercise more intensely in one workout than in another. This practice allows the body to adapt and become stronger more rapidly than training at maximal intensities for all exercises during every weight training session.

   People interested in achieving high levels of strength should incorporate base and peak cycles into their training strategy. Base (or load) cycles are characterized by high volume with varying intensities, while peak cycles employ low volume and high-intensity workouts with plenty of rest. Peak cycles are designed to produce maximum performance efficiency. The base or load cycle is the foundation for peak performance. However, peak fitness can only be maintained for short periods of time; every peak is gained at the price of some deconditioning. Both cycles are important. The successes of the peaks make the hard work of the base period worthwhile.

7. **Don't overtrain.** This principle is one of the most difficult to adhere to because it goes against the work ethic that is ingrained in so many people. Think of conditioning as a long-term process. Adaptations to training take place gradually. Excessive training tends to lead to overtraining and overuse injuries rather than accelerated development of fitness.

8. **Train systematically.** Plan an approximate workout schedule for the coming months (or even for the next year). Of course, do not be so rigid that you can't change the program to accommodate unforeseen circumstances. The important thing is that you have a plan, so you can comfortably apply the stress of exercise in a manner that will produce a consistent increase in fitness.

   Coaching, training partners, and a training diary will help your workouts become more systematic. Coaching helps you meet your competitive goals. A good coach is knowledgeable and experienced and can keep you from making common training mistakes. He or she will help motivate you. Training partners are also important for motivation and competition. It is a lot easier to make it to your workout if you are accountable to someone. A training partner will share the agony and ecstasy that accompanies training. The training diary will allow you to formulate your goals and help you keep track of which training techniques work for you and which don't work. A description of the training diary appears in Chapter 2.

9. **Train your mind.** This is one of the most difficult skills to acquire, but is critical for attaining high levels of physical fitness. It is thoroughly interrelated with the physical aspect of training because "the body will conform if the mind is willing." Physically fit people and successful athletes must believe in themselves and their potential, have goals, and know how to achieve these goals. Attaining physical fitness is extremely difficult and is an ongoing process—you need the proper "mind set" in order to achieve your goal.

10. **Become a student of your sport.** This may be the most important training principle. If you become an "educated sports person," you

will plan and carry out your program intelligently. You will not be as liable to jump into every training fad that comes along, and you will always be in control of your own training program. Learn everything you can about training, and you will get the most from your exercise program.

11. **Keep the exercise program in its proper perspective.** Too often, people think of themselves solely as aerobic dancers, body builders, football players, runners, cyclists, or swimmers, rather than as the human beings who participate in those activities. While sports are important, you must also have time for your family and other important aspects of your life. Leading a well-rounded life will not diminish your chances for success and will make your training program more enjoyable.

References

Armstrong, R.B. Mechanisms of exercise-induced delayed onset muscular soreness: A brief review. *Med. Sci. Sports Exerc.* 16:529–538, 1984.

Atha, J. Strengthening muscle. *Exercise and Sport Sciences Reviews* 9:1–73, 1981.

Brooks, G.A. and T.D. Fahey. *Exercise Physiology: Human Bioenergetics and Its Applications.* New York, NY: Macmillan, 1984.

Brooks, G.A. and T.D. Fahey. *Fundamentals of Human Performance.* New York, NY: Macmillan, 1987.

Costill, D.L., E.F. Coyle, W.F. Fink, G.R. Lesmes, and F.A. Witzmann. Adaptations in skeletal muscle following strength training. *J. Appl. Physiol.* 46:96–99, 1979.

Dons, B., K. Bollerup, F. Bonde–Petersen, and S. Hancke. The effect of weight-lifting exercise related to muscle fiber composition and muscle cross-sectional area in humans. *Eur. J. Appl. Physiol.* 40:95–106, 1979.

Edgerton, V.R. Mammalian muscle fiber types and their adaptability. *Amer. Zool.* 18:113–125, 1978

Fahey, T.D. (Ed.) *Athletic Training: Principles and Practice.* Mountain View, Ca.: Mayfield Publishing, 1986.

Fahey, T.D., L. Akka, and R. Rolph. Body composition and VO$_2$max of exceptional weight–trained athletes. *J. Appl. Physiol.* 39:559–561, 1975.

Fleck, S.J. and W.J. Kraemer. Resistance training: Physiological responses and adaptations. *Physician and Sports Med.* 16:108–124, 1988.

Goldberg, A.L. Mechanisms of growth and atrophy of skeletal muscle. in: Cassens, R.G. (Ed.). *Muscle Biology.* New York, NY: Marcel Dekker, Inc., 1972.

Gonyea, W.J. Role of exercise in inducing increases in skeletal muscle fiber number. *J. Appl. Physiol.* 48:421–426, 1980.

Gonyea, W.J., and D. Sale. Physiology of weight lifting. *Arch. Phys. Med. Rehabil.* 63:235–237, 1982.

Hickson, R.C. Interference of strength development by simultaneously training for strength and endurance. Eur. J. Appl. Physiol. 45:255–263, 1980.

Ho, K.W., R.R. Roy, C.D. Tweedle, W.W. Heusner, W.D. Van Huss, and R.E. Carrow. Skeletal muscle fiber splitting with weight–lifting exercise in rats. *Amer. J. Anat.* 157:433–440, 1980.

Lesmes, G.R., D. Costill, E.F. Coyle, and W.J. Fink. Muscle strength and power changes during maximal isokinetic training. *Med. Sci. Sports* 10:266–269, 1978.

MacDougall, J.D., G.R. Ward, D.G. Sale, and J.R. Sutton. Biochemical adaptation of human skeletal muscle to heavy resistance training and immobilization. *J. Appl. Physiol.* 43:700–703, 1977.

Moritani, T. and H.A. deVries. Potential for gross muscle hypertrophy in older men. *J. Gerontology* 35:672–682, 1980.

O'Shea, P. Effects of selected weight training programs on the development of strength and muscle hypertrophy. *Research Quarterly* 37:95–102, 1964.

Staron, R.S., F.C. Hagerman, and R.S. Hikida. The effects of detraining on an elite power lifter. *J. Neurological Sciences* 51:247–257, 1981.

Thorstensson, A. Muscle strength, fibre types, and enzyme activities in man. *Acta Physiol. Scand.* 443(Suppl.):1–45, 1976.

CHAPTER TWO

▼

Starting Your Program

Numerous training techniques increase strength. To the beginner, the choices may seem almost mind-boggling. Training techniques go by such exotic names as isometrics, isokinetics, and isotonics, and they often employ exercise devices that look like something from a medieval torture chamber. However, all of these devices and techniques have one thing in common: they provide increased resistance to muscle contractions. Muscles respond to increased tension by growing stronger and, often, larger. In this chapter we will examine the characteristics of various training techniques and discuss the basics of formulating a weight training program suited to you.

TYPES OF WEIGHT TRAINING EXERCISES

People who weight train are interested in at least one of three of its effects on the body: (1) an increase in muscular strength, (2) an increase in muscular power, and (3) a change in the muscles' shape or size. Strength is the ability to exert force; power is work per unit of time. In other words, power is the ability to exert force rapidly, and in most sports, power is more important than strength. Fortunately, there is a transfer between strength and power—exercises that develop strength also tend to develop power. Many athletes spend long hours developing strength in the weight room in the hope of increasing power for their sport. For example, tennis players often do exercises, such as bench presses or lat pulls, in order to serve and hit the ball harder. The players lift weights at much slower speeds than they play tennis, yet the strength they gain during the relatively slow weight training exercises increases their power in the faster tennis movements.

There are two kinds of strength exercises: **isometric** (static) and **isotonic** (dynamic). Isometric exercise involves applying force without movement, while isotonic exercise is applying force with movement. These exercises can be executed concentrically or eccentrically. A **concentric muscle contraction** occurs when the muscle exerts force as it shortens. This occurs during the pushing phase of a weight training exercise. In an **eccentric muscle contraction**, force is exerted as the muscle lengthens. This begins when the weight is lowered to begin the pushing phase of the exercise.

Isometric Exercise

Isometric exercise is a static muscle contraction involving no movement. An immovable object, such as a fixed bar or wall, is used as resistance. Although isometric exercise received considerable attention in the late 1950s, it is now less popular as a primary means of gaining strength. Isometric exercise does not increase strength throughout a joint's range of motion (unless practiced at various points in the range of motion); strength gains from isometrics occur only at or near the joint angle where the exercise was practiced. Likewise, isometric training does not improve (and may hamper) the ability to exert force rapidly (that is, gain power). In addition, performing excessive amounts of isometric exercise may lead to injury.

Weight trainers occasionally use isometrics to overcome "sticking points" in an exercise's range of motion. For example, people who have difficulty pushing weights from their chest during the bench press may perform the exercise isometrically at the point where they are experiencing the greatest degree of difficulty. A power rack is sometimes used for this type of isometric training (Figure 2–1).

Contracting the muscles without moving them, such as tightening the abdominal muscles, is a type of isometric exercise that is valuable for toning and strengthening muscles, especially when recovering from an injury. These useful exercises can be practiced almost anywhere and do not require any equipment. Examples of isometric exercises useful for strengthening the lower back and abdomen appear in Chapters 5 and 6, respectively.

Isotonic Exercise

Isotonic exercises, which are muscle contractions resulting in movement, are the most popular type of weight training with most people. Most exer-

Figure 2–1 *The power rack. This device is used to help overcome "sticking points."*

cises using barbells, dumbbells, weight machines, and the body's own weight (for example, push-ups) are isotonic. Isotonic techniques include: constant resistance, variable resistance exercise, eccentric loading, plyometrics, speed loading, and isokinetic exercise.

Constant Resistance Constant resistance exercise uses a constant load, such as a barbell or dumbbell throughout the range of motion, and is the most common form of weight training. The relative resistance of the load varies with the angle of the joint, so that it is usually easier to move the weight at the end of the range of motion than at the beginning. Maximum loading occurs only at the weakest point in the range of motion.

Variable Resistance Variable resistance exercise involves increasing the load throughout the range of motion so that there is a more consistent stress on the muscles. This form of exercise requires special weight machines that vary the resistance while the exercise is performed. Variable resistance places more stress on the muscles at the end of the range of motion, a position of increased mechanical advantage. Sports scientists have not yet determined whether or not this form of training is superior to constant resistance exercise. However, years of experience by weight-lifters, body-builders, and other strength-trained athletes suggest that constant resistance exercise is better for building strength and muscle size.

Eccentric Loading As discussed earlier, eccentric loading occurs when the muscle contracts as it lengthens. Muscles contract eccentrically whenever a weight is lowered into position prior to lifting it. Eccentric muscle contraction is vital in training because it allows you to control a weight. If your body were incapable of contracting muscles eccentrically, controlled movement of your body would be impossible. The active phase of most weight training exercises (lifting the weight) is concentric. However, exercises can also be performed solely eccentrically, a type of training popularly referred to as "negatives." Eccentric loading is an effective way to gain strength, although it is inferior to other isotonic techniques.

One drawback of eccentric loading is that it seems to cause more muscle soreness than other methods. The high tensions generated during this technique cause small tears in the muscle that result in muscle soreness a day or two after the workout. Strength athletes avoid this method as a primary training technique but often use it as an adjunct to other training methods.

Plyometrics Sometimes called implosion training, plyometrics is the sudden eccentric loading and stretching of muscles followed by their forceful concentric contraction. The sudden stretch activates receptors within the muscles and the muscles' own elasticity to react and cause a more vigorous contraction. An example of plyometrics is jumping from a bench to the ground and then jumping back onto the bench (Figure 2–2). Plyometrics should be practiced to develop the specifically desired type of power. For example, for developing vertical power to increase jumping capacity, perform plyometric exercises in a vertical direction. Practicing highly repetitive plyometrics will develop muscle strength and endurance. Plyometrics have become very popular with many athletes, but research is still needed to determine if this training technique is safe and effective.

Speed Loading Speed loading involves moving a weight as rapidly as possible in an attempt to approach the movement velocities used in athletic maneuvers such as throwing a baseball or sprinting. For gaining strength, weight training at ordinary speeds is superior to speed loading.

Figure 2–2 *Plyometrics. This type of isotonic exercise overloads the muscles' elastic component, which results in a forceful muscle contraction. The technique is practiced to improve strength and power. A technique for developing leg power involves (a and b) jumping off a low bench, (c) landing on the floor and absorbing the shock with the legs, and (d) jumping back up onto the bench.*

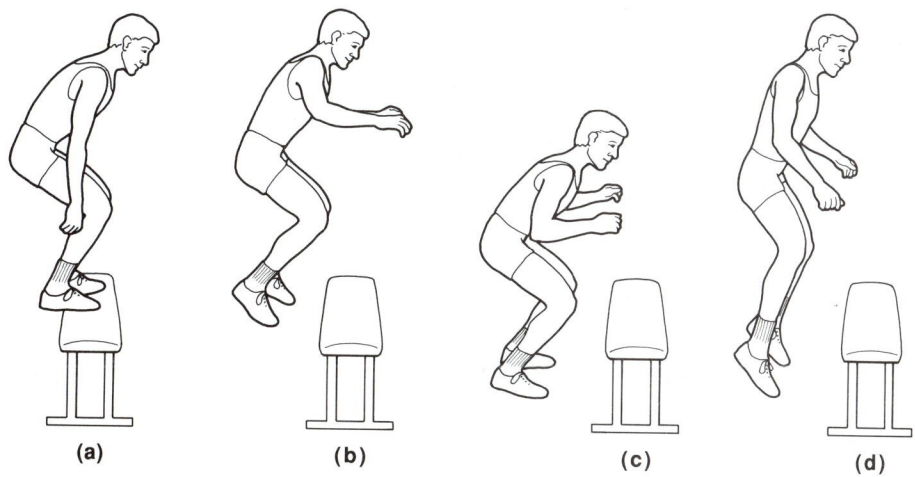

(a) **(b)** **(c)** **(d)**

Speed loading prevents the muscles from creating sufficient tension to cause a training effect. Strength athletes, such as football players, often practice this technique at various times throughout their training schedules in the hope of achieving maximum power. There may be an advantage to attempting to lift heavy loads rapidly. Such a training strategy may increase muscular power.

Isokinetic Exercise Isokinetic exercise, also called accommodating resistance exercise, involves muscle contraction at a constant speed. The exerted force is resisted by an equal force from the isokinetic machine. Resistance is provided only when force is actively applied, so this type of training is often considered to be safer than other forms of resistive exercise. Isokinetic devices allow simultaneous training and the measurement of strength during relatively fast movements. Proponents of isokinetic exercise say that the ability to train at faster speeds results in a training effect more specific to the rapid movements used in sports. Isokinetic muscle loading is also used mainly by therapists in the assessment and treatment of injuries. Several weight training equipment manufacturers use isokinetic loading in their strength training machines. These machines tend to be considerably more expensive than traditional weight training equipment, so they are not as widely available.

Proprioceptive Neuromuscular Facilitation (PNF)

PNF is manual resistance exercise that uses a combination of stretching, isotonic, and isometric loading. This technique is widely used by physical therapists to develop strength and flexibility in injured patients. As yet, it is not commonly used by athletes or the general population for improving physical fitness.

FORMULATING A PROGRAM

There are many considerations when starting a weight training program including program goals and structure, proper training techniques, and safety.

Determining Program Goals

Countless combinations of weight training exercises and training philosophies exist. The right one for you depends on your goals. For example, if your goal is to become a champion body-builder, your program will be much different than if you want to condition yourself for football or improve your physical appearance. There are training programs appropriate for every goal. As discussed in Chapter 1, it is best to begin the program performing many repetitions of each exercise before attempting maximum loads. This is true regardless of your ultimate goal. Specific programs for a variety of program goals appear in Appendix 2.

Developing Strength and Power Weight training is the best activity for developing strength and power. In strength–speed sports—such as football, the throwing events in track and field, and competitive weight lifting—strength and power are critical components for success.

The weight training programs of strength–speed athletes typically center on three types of weight lifting exercises: presses, pulls, and multi-joint lower body exercises. Presses include the bench press, incline press, military press, seated press, push press, jerks, and dumbbell press. Pulls include cleans, snatches, high pulls, and dead lifts. Multijoint lower body exercises include squats, leg presses, hack squats, and rack squats. In general, relatively heavy loads (70–100 percent of your maximum) and a moderate number of repetitions (1–8 times) are used in an effort to achieve maximum strength and power. Auxiliary exercises to develop arm, back, abdominal, calf, and neck muscle strength (depending on the sport) are also practiced, but presses, pulls, and multijoint lower body exercises constitute the core of the program.

Strength–speed athletes have many training philosophies. Traditional programs often involve training three days per week, using as much weight as possible for each lift, and completing an identical set of exercises during each session. Experienced athletes and coaches have found that performing all three types of strength–speed exercises during each workout hinders recovery, leads to overtraining, and hampers optimal progress. As discussed in Chapter 1, the use of cycle training (that is, periodization of training), in which exercises and training volumes and intensities vary between workouts and between different times of year, speeds up progress. Cycle training will be described in greater detail later in this chapter.

Developing a Healthy-looking Body While beauty is in the eye of the beholder, several goals are common to many people. For women, these may include having a lean, shapely body. Men also want lean, shapely bodies but also tend to desire more muscle mass. Several major principles for developing a lean, athletic-looking body apply to competitive body builders as well as to those men and women who are interested in improving their health and appearance.

The first principle is to *minimize body fat*. Discussed in detail in Chapter 8, the control of body fat is determined by an energy balance: if more energy (food) is consumed than is expended (metabolism and exercise), then fat is gained; conversely, fat is lost when energy expenditure exceeds energy intake. Body fat may be controlled by eating a well-balanced diet containing adequate but not excessive calories (energy) and by participating in aerobic exercise in addition to the weight training program.

While having only a small effect on energy balance, weight training exercises can improve the appearance of certain parts of the body, particularly the abdomen. This occurs because the exercises increase muscle tone, which makes the body part look tighter. However, even though the body part may look better, the fat will remain unless you shift the overall energy balance. There is no such thing as spot reducing: you cannot lose fat in a specific area of the body by exercising nearby muscles.

The second principle is to *build muscle size using high intensity exercise*. Large muscles develop because they are subjected to heavy loads during training (that is, high degrees of muscle tension). Body builders often overemphasize workouts involving many sets and many repetitions (recall that a repetition is one performance of the exercise; a set is a group of repetitions followed by rest). While these workouts are essential for defining muscle shape, they are less effective for developing muscle size. Consequently, a certain proportion of the body-builder's training program should be devoted to high intensity, low to moderate number of repetition (2–6 repetitions per set) workouts. As discussed before, programs designed to produce muscle bulk will be less effective in women than men.

The third principle is to *develop muscle definition by doing high set, high repetition workouts*. Muscle definition is the elusive property of muscles that allows their structure (that is, ripples) to be defined and seen more clearly. For example, defined abdominal muscles often look like a washboard. High numbers of repetitions, high numbers of set exercise routines are of limited value in improving muscle definition if you have excessive body fat.

Improving Sports Performance The principle of specificity states that the body adapts according to the stresses placed upon it. Each sport has specific physical demands. The golfer needs strong forearms and back and leg muscles, while the pitcher needs strong legs and shoulder muscles. The leg strength requirements of the alpine skier are considerably different from those of the cross-country skier. The weight training routine must be structured to meet the needs of the sport.

It is important to focus on the muscles and joints that are commonly subjected to injury in a particular sport. For example, the "rotator cuff" muscles in pitchers, tennis players, and swimmers are particularly vulnerable to injury. Unfortunately, these muscles are seldom conditioned in a loosely structured weight training program unless they are injured. It makes a lot more sense to condition vulnerable joints and muscles to prevent injury.

Three major weight training principles to practice for increasing strength for sports are:

1. *Identify and train those muscles and joints that are particularly effective in the activity*

2. *Identify and train those muscles and joints that are prone to injury in the activity*

3. *Maintain a high level of fitness in all of the major muscle groups of the body*

Weight Training as Part of a General Conditioning Program Fitness has many components including endurance, strength, power, speed, agility, flexibility, balance, and absence of disease. Each of these components has value in particular sports or physical activities. For example, a person may have excellent endurance on a ski slope but have poor endurance on the running track or in the swimming pool. So, to be fit for a variety of physical activities, you have to practice those activities. Regular participation in weight, flexibility, and endurance training will carry over into most of the activities of daily life and will improve performance in them.

It is almost impossible to remain optimally fit for all the activities that people enjoy. It is difficult to do regular conditioning exercises, ski, hike, swim, play tennis, volleyball, golf, and windsurf several times a week while also working or attending school. You must make compromises. It is better to choose a few exercises to do regularly than to select an overambitious program that cannot be maintained. The general conditioning program, designed to prepare you for an active lifestyle and foster good health, should contain the following components:

▶ **Endurance exercise.** This type of exercise is perhaps the most essential part of any conditioning program because it affects the heart and circulation and can help prevent heart disease. A general endurance exercise plan is to participate in large muscle endurance activities—such as running, walking, cycling, or swimming—3–5 times per week at over 60 percent of your maximum capacity for 20–60 continuous minutes.

▶ **Flexibility exercise.** Flexibility or stretching exercises are important for maintaining the normal range of motion of the major joints of the body. These exercises should be performed at least five times per week. A minimal program should include stretches for the hamstrings (back of the thigh), quadriceps (front of the thigh), Achilles tendons, groin (inside of the thigh), back, and shoulders. Stretches should be practiced statically: stretch to the point of tightness in the muscle.

Never "bounce" during stretching exercises.   ◀ CAUTION

▶ **Weight training.** A basic weight training program should be practiced 2–4 days per week, working the major major muscle groups. The program should include exercises for the shoulders, chest, arms, abdomen, back, and legs. Workouts should last 30–60 minutes.

▶ **Specific skills.** Conditioning is much easier if it is included as part of an activity you enjoy. For example, cross-country skiing is a terrific conditioning activity that many people find more enjoyable than running. While it isn't a practical activity for most people to do on a regular basis, it can be a substitute for running while you are on vacation. Likewise, sports such as tennis, golf, volleyball, alpine skiing, waterskiing, and windsurfing provide a good conditioning effect and can be used to supplement the exercise program. Sports skills are valuable because they often contribute to all the components of fitness and tend to be more enjoyable than exercises used merely for conditioning.

Be as active as you can be. Participate in as many activities as time allows, but don't get stuck in a rut or overemphasize only one component of fitness. Too many people either weight train or run, forgeting about the other areas of fitness.

The Structure of a Weight Training Program

The structure of your weight training program depends on your goals. Many body builders train 4–6 hours per day, 5–6 days per week. Competitive weight-lifters or football players practice complicated lifts such as snatches, clean and jerk, and also train for many hours. These practices are unnecessary for the individual simply interested in general fitness.

Beginning the Program First, determine if weight training is an appropriate activity for you. If you are younger than 35 years old and in good health, there is probably no reason not to enter into a weight training program. If you are over 35 years old or have health problems—particularly those involving high blood pressure, heart disease, stroke, obesity, or musculoskeletal disorders—you should consult a physician before starting an exercise program.

Second, find a good place to train. If you are not enrolled in a class, either purchase your own equipment for home use or join a gym. Home gyms are a sound alternative because after you have paid for the equipment, you own it and there are few additional expenses. Also, because the equipment is close at hand, you may be more apt to use it more often. On the other hand, weight equipment has a way of ending up in the closet, forgotten. Home equipment can also present a safety hazard because often there may be no one home to spot for you while you exercise.

Never weight train without a spotter!   ◄ CAUTION

Commercial health clubs offer many advantages that are difficult to match with the home gym. Clubs often provide sophisticated and expensive equipment that would be impossible for most individuals to acquire for their homes. In addition, gyms provide a pleasant atmosphere that is conducive to training and associating with people whose goals are similar to your own. Other people often provide inspiration and incentive for you to train harder. Thus, you may progress faster in a health club than you would in a home gym.

Health clubs also have their drawbacks. Some are often crowded, and the equipment is sometimes in disrepair. Occasionally, health club managers are unscrupulous and will talk you into signing membership contracts that are not in your best interests. Health clubs are not always financially stable. It is not unusual to pay for a multi-year membership one week and find that the club has gone out of business the next. Be a knowledgeable and wary consumer. Join a gym that provides good value for your money and the atmosphere you want.

Number of Training Sessions Per Week Most people should train between 2–4 days per week, with 3 days per week being most popular. Two days per week is the minimum involvement necessary to improve strength. Training fewer days leads to regular muscle soreness and injury.

Excessive training is also a bad idea. Training too often leads to overtraining and delayed progress. Studies show heavy training days invariably lead to tissue damage. Damaged tissue needs time to recover before the next intense session.

Four-day-a-week programs are popular with some athletes during peak seasons dedicated to conditioning. Typically, they will work the upper body two days per week and the lower body the other two days per week. For example, Monday and Thursday would be devoted to training the upper body, and Tuesday and Friday to the lower body.

More is not necessarily better. Training intensity is perhaps the primary factor determining increased strength. A person who trains too often and too hard never recovers enough to train intensely. Sometimes it is better to rest than to train.

Choosing the Correct Starting Weight It is always better to err on the side of safety. For the first set, choose a weight that you can move easily for at least ten repetitions. Again, a repetition is one performance of the exercise, while a set is a group of repetitions followed by a rest. Don't push it during the first few workouts, or you will experience muscle soreness. Recent studies suggest that muscle soreness (soreness experienced 1–2 days after a workout) is caused by tissue damage. During subsequent training sessions, add weight gradually until you are bearing a significant load and the ten-repetition set becomes difficult.

Add weight when you can finish each set with relative ease. If you feel as though you can do 11 or 12 repetitions with a particular weight, it's time to add more resistance. If after adding weight you can only do 8–9 repetitions, stay with that weight until you can again complete the 10 repetitions per set. On the other hand, if after adding weight you can only do 4–6 repetitions, then you have added too much weight and some must be removed.

Experienced weight trainers must be beware of using too much weight after a layoff. Muscle soreness and injury will result if you try to resume your program where you left off. As described in Chapter 1, getting in shape gradually is a basic principle of training. Excessive training loads do not encourage the body to adapt faster; they only cause injury and delayed progress.

Warm-up Most experts agree that warm-up is essential before exercise. Empirical evidence suggests that warm-up improves performance and prevents injury. Warm-up raises body temperature so that the muscles respond better. It increases tissue elasticity (making it less prone to injury) and promotes joint lubrication. In addition, intense exercise without warm-up may place the heart at risk.

Warm-up can be either general or specific. General warm-up involves the whole body—large muscle exercises such as jumping jacks, stretching, running in place, or stationary cycling. Specific warm-up involves performing the same lift that you intend to begin with in your program but using a weight considerably below your normal training level. For example, a person who is about to perform 3 sets of 10 repetitions of 200 lbs bench presses might perform 2 sets of 10 repetitions at 100 lbs as a warm-up. Similar warm-up exercises would be performed for each major lift that makes up the program.

Sets and Repetitions The ideal number of repetitions and sets is determined by your goals. In general, if you desire increased endurance, do more repetitions and sets. If your primary goal is increased strength, do fewer repetitions and use more weight.

Research has shown that the 4–6 repetitions per set for 3–5 sets is best for developing strength. People who are interested in achieving single maximum lifts must occasionally do 1–3 repetition sets, so that they can adjust to the heavier weights. Experienced weight trainers use a variety of combinations of sets and repetitions. Some of these will be discussed in the section on cycling that appears later in this chapter.

Beginners should start off with more repetitions and lighter weights at the beginning of a training program. This gives tissues a chance to adjust to increased muscular loading and minimizes the chances of injury. At first, it is best to do 3 sets of 10 repetitions of about 6–8 exercises. Practice this program, gradually increasing the weight, for at least two months before decreasing the number of repetitions in each set. An example of a modest beginning weight training program appears in Table 2–1.

A number of training systems use a technique called **pyramiding**, which contains a built-in warm-up. Basically, an exercise is practiced for three or more sets, increasing the weight during each set. This technique was originally introduced by T.L. DeLorme in the 1950s. Delorme recommended three sets of ten repetitions of each exercise with resistance progressively increasing from 50 to 75 percent and finally 100 percent of

Table 2–1 Example of a Beginning Weight Training Program

Exercise	Sets	Repetitions
Bench press	3	10
Lat pulls	3	10
Lateral raise	3	10
Biceps curls	3	10
Triceps extensions	3	10
Abdominal curls	3	10
Squats	3	10
Calf raises	3	10

Table 2–2 Examples of Selected Weight–Set–Repetition Methods

Circuit Training

Six to twenty exercise stations are established in the series.The individual progresses from one station to the next, either performing a given number of repetitions or doing as many repetitions as possible during a time period (for example, 20 seconds).

Constant Set Method

After warm-up, the same weight and number of sets and repetitions are used for the exercise. Example:

Bench press 5 sets of 5 repetitions at 200 lbs.

DeLorme Method

Three sets of 10 repetitions at 50, 75, and 100 percent of maximum. Example for the bench press for a person who can do 10 repetitions at 150 lbs:

Set 1	10 repetitions	75 lbs (50%)
Set 2	10 repetitions	112.5 lbs (75%)
Set 3	10 repetitions	150 lbs (100%)

Pyramid Method

Uses multiple progressive sets. May be ascending or ascending–descending.

(continued)

maximum capacity (10 RM; ten "repetitions maximum," the maximum weight that can be lifted for ten repetitions).

Many systems for regulating the amount of weights lifted during training have been introduced including the constant set method, failure method, circuit training, and super sets. Some of these techniques reduce the weight during subsequent sets after reaching the maximum weight. Any technique you choose should allow you to warm-up before you subject your muscles to an increased load. Selected techniques are described in Table 2–2.

		Table 2–2 (continued)		

Ascending pyramid

Set 1	5 repetitions	150 lbs
Set 2	5 repetitions	175 lbs
Set 3	5 repetitions	200 lbs

Ascending-descending pyramid

Set 1	5 repetitions	150 lbs
Set 2	5 repetitions	175 lbs
Set 3	5 repetitions	200 lbs
Set 4	5 repetitions	175 lbs
Set 5	5 repetitions	150 lbs

Super Sets

Usually uses two exercises, typically with opposing muscle groups, in rapid succession. Example:

Set 1	10 repetitions	50 lbs	knee extensions
Set 1	10 repetitions	30 lbs	knee flexions
Rest			
Set 2	10 repetitions	50 lbs	knee extensions
Set 2	10 repetitions	30 lbs	knee flexions
Rest			
Repeat			

Basic Cycling Techniques (Periodization of Training) Many people typically go to the gym 3–5 days a week and "kill" themselves doing the same lifts with as much weight as they can handle. While hard work is a cornerstone of progress in any program, it is worthless unless it is applied correctly. A training program, or single workout, is misdirected unless it causes the body to adapt as rapidly as possible and to improve its function or its appearance. Misdirected hard work results in overtraining and is counterproductive. Overtraining keeps you from reaching your goal. Many elite athletes use a powerful technique called periodization of training or cycle training. This technique allows the body to adapt rapidly without overtraining. Cycle training actually prepares your body to accept and benefit from intense workouts.

Periodization of training is a technique that varies the type, volume, and intensity of the training throughout the year. For example, in athletics the year is often divided into general preparatory, specialized preparatory, early competitive, and main competitive stages. Each stage is characterized by specific forms of training. The general preparatory phase (sometimes called active rest) involves rest from the athlete's principal activity but maintenance of fitness through participation in complementary sports. The specialized preparatory stage (also called the load cycle) is typically devoted to developing base fitness for the event and usually involves high volume and moderate intensity training. Finally, the competitive phases (also called peak cycles) are dedicated to advancing peak performance and usually involve high intensity and moderate volume training with increasing rest as critical competitions near.

Each major cycle contains microcycles in which the volume, intensity, and rest vary from workout to workout or from week to week. The purpose of these microcycles is to allow muscle systems adequate recovery time. According to several studies, intensity (either in terms of absolute load or absolute volume) is the chief factor in enhancing fitness. In traditional training programs, athletes train hard almost every session, which may lead to overtraining. Microcycles prepare athletes for intense training days by ensuring that they have recovered enough to train maximally.

Periodization of training encourages your body to adapt systematically with a minimum risk of injury. Small gains are made over a long period of time. The system is designed to improve fitness, so that peak performance occurs at a predetermined time in the season. Part of the basis for the cycle training method is that individuals adapt better to changing stimuli than to a constant program. While much of this is undoubtedly due to the rapid learning that occurs when a new activity is introduced, certainly the change in activities with each new cycle is psychologically stimulating.

Considerable muscle and connective tissue damage occurs during and after intense endurance or strength training. While the relationship between tissue healing rate and the structure of the training program is not known, common sense tells us that there is such a relationship. It is probable that muscle fibers must heal to some extent before they can be safely subjected to additional maximal stress.

Cycling techniques are ideal for people pursuing general conditioning. It is not necessary to do the same exercises every session using the same weights. Vary your program. Do some exercises intensely during one workout and other exercises intensely during the next. A basic three-days-

Table 2–3 An Example of Cycle Training for General Conditioning

The exercises are described in Chapters 3–7.

Exercise	Sets	Repetitions	Weight (lbs)
Monday			
Bench press	4	10	150
Lat pulls	3	10	90
Squats	4	10	175
Abdominal curls	3	20	—
Back extensions	3	15	—
Arm curls	3	10	60
Triceps ext.	3	10	35
Wednesday			
Incline press	3	10	100
Pull-ups	5	5	—
Pull-overs	3	10	40
Leg press	3	10	275 (machine)
Calf raises	4	20	275 (machine)
Abdominal curls	3	40	—
Good mornings	3	10	35
Friday			
Bench press	3	10	130
Lat pulls	3	10	110
Squats	3	10	150
Abdominal curls	3	20	—
Back extensions	3	15	—
Arm curls	4	10	70
Triceps ext.	4	10	40

per-week program designed for general conditioning that uses cycling is shown in Table 2–3. This program uses different lifts with varying intensities in each of the three training sessions. Cycling makes the program more interesting and speeds recovery between sessions.

Making Steady Progress Initially, gains seem to come easily, but every weight trainer will reach a point where progress becomes difficult. Because the body adapts rapidly at first, many of the gains are due as much to learning new exercises as to actual changes in the muscles. The best thing to do when you are "on the shelf" (not improving any more) is to examine your program. Lack of improvement is usually caused by overtraining, undertraining, or following an inflexible program. If you work very hard every training session and never miss a workout and are still not making any progress, then maybe you are doing too much. Try cycling your workouts or take a week or two off. Rest can do amazing things—often you can expect to return to personal records in the weight room if you just take a brief rest.

On the other hand, some people don't work hard enough. Are you going through the full motions when you train? Try adding more weight for at least one set of each exercise, even if it causes you to do fewer repetitions. Make sure you complete each workout. If you cut a few exercises out of the program each session, that can amount to a lot of work after a few weeks.

Many people get enough rest, complete their workouts, but still fail to progress. Then the answer is to change the nature of the program. The body adapts quickly to exercises at first but slows after the first month or so. You can often begin to make progress again by changing your program. Do exercises that are slightly different from the ones you usually do. For example, if you do barbell bench presses as your major press, substitute dumbbell bench presses and incline presses. The power rack (see Figure 2–1) can be used to help overcome sticking points. Sometimes, having a spotter assist you so that you can use more weight will help get you over the hump. If you are doing normal grip bench presses, change your grip and do the exercise with a narrower or wider grip. Another effective technique is to add exercises that strengthen muscles needed for the primary exercises. For example, doing bar dips with weight is effective in improving the bench press. Dips strengthen the triceps, which are essential to the bench press. Leg extensions will improve the squat. Change the nature of the exercise stress, and your body will again adapt more quickly.

Integrating a Weight Training Program with Other Sports and Exercises Intense weight training can be exhausting and can interfere with the performance of other activities. After a vigorous weight training session, you may be more susceptible to injury if you immediately participate in another sport. If possible, get plenty of rest after an intense workout before participating in a sport where you might be susceptible to injury. If most of your program consists of general conditioning exercises, schedule strength and endurance exercises on different days. At least schedule intense weight training on light endurance training days.

Cool-down The purpose of cool-down is to return muscle temperatures and metabolic rate to normal levels. Cool-down after weight training, unlike after endurance exercise, consists of relaxing and maybe talking to friends. In contrast, after endurance exercise, it is important to gradually wind down the tempo of activity. Because weight training is not a continuous activity, it is not necessary to perform progressively lower intensity activities at the end of a workout session. Nevertheless, it is critical that you don't shower immediately after a vigorous weight training session. During intense weight training, blood is shunted to the muscles, and hormones are mobilized to help you perform heightened physical activity. Taking a hot shower immediately after exercise places stress on the heart that may not be tolerated by some people. Give yourself at least 5–10 minutes to relax after a workout before showering.

TECHNIQUE AND SAFETY

Weight training is a highly enjoyable activity that offers tremendous rewards. However, a weight room can be a dangerous place. There are obstructions to trip over, crushing weights that can fall on you, and devices that can pinch you. Carelessness with weight training equipment can lead to injury or even death. Always observe basic safety principles to ensure that your weight training experience is a good one.

Clothing

You will not want to wear street clothes in a weight room because they may be ruined by sweat, oil, and dirt. The workout clothing you choose should allow enough freedom to perform the exercises but not be so loose that it gets caught in the exercise machines. Almost any standard exercise clothing will do. These should include a t-shirt, shorts, socks, and training shoes. Women might consider using a sports bra for added support.

Shoes If your program includes squats and pulling exercises, such as cleans and snatches, it is best to use either weight lifting shoes, or heavy shoes that provide good support. Weight lifting shoes can be purchased from weight lifting supply stores. Most major athletic shoe companies manufacture weight lifting shoes, so they can be ordered if the local sports store doesn't carry them.

Weight Lifting Belt A weight lifting belt is worn by serious weight trainers for back protection. Many experts feel that the belts help maintain proper spinal alignment when handling heavy weights. While a belt may be helpful during any exercise, it is particularly important to wear one when doing squats and pulling exercises. The effectiveness of weight lifting belts has not been studied scientifically.

CAUTION ▶   Don't rely solely on a belt to protect your back. Good
lifting technique and strong, flexible muscles are
critical for preventing back injury.

Wraps Many advanced weight trainers use wraps to support their knees, wrists, or elbows. Wraps support injured joints or provide extra support. Wrapping material includes elastic bandages, leather, and neoprene. They are unnecessary for most people involved in general conditioning weight training programs.

Some people use wraps to counteract knee pain during or after weight training sessions. While there are many causes of knee pain, it is often caused by excessive compression of the knee cap on the underlying bone (femur). Knee wraps may increase this compression and make the pain worse. A solution is to purchase a knee wrap that has a hole built in for the knee cap. This will provide support, while reducing compression on the knee cap.

Grip wraps are strips of cotton webbing (such as that used on army belts or karate belts) that are wrapped around the wrist and barbell for the purpose of increasing grip strength during pulling lifts such as cleans, dead lifts, and snatches. The grip is often the limiting factor in these lifts, and improving grip strength allows the use of more weight during workouts. Wraps are used mainly by advanced weight trainers.

Gloves Gloves protect your hands during weight training. Barbells and dumbbels are knurled to aid gripping, but the knurls are abrasive. To prevent rough and calloused hands, gloves may be the answer.

SAFETY RULES
FOR WEIGHT TRAINING

Weight training can be dangerous if safety guidelines are not followed. The following are basic principles for preventing injuries in the weight room.

▶ Be aware of what is going on around you.

▶ Stay away from other people when they are busy doing exercises. Bumping into them could result in injury.

▶ Use spotters in any exercise in which you can conceivably lose control of the weight. Spotters should also use proper lifting techniques.

▶ Always use collars on barbells and dumbbells.

▶ Don't use more weight than you are capable of handling safely.

▶ Report any equipment malfunctions immediately.

▶ Protect your back by observing proper lifting techniques and by using a weight lifting belt when performing heavy lifts.

▶ Don't hold your breath while performing exercises.

▶ Always warm-up before training.

▶ Don't exercise if you are ill.

Preventing Accidents

Accidents and injuries do happen in weight training. Maximum physical effort, elaborate machinery, rapid movements, and heavy weights can combine to make the weight room a dangerous place if proper precautions are not taken.

Spotters

CAUTION ▶   Use spotters whenever there is the danger
of a person missing a lift and being caught under
the fallen weight.

Spotters assist the lifter in the event of a failed repetition, help the lifter move the weight into position to begin a lift, and actively assist with the lift.

Helping with the weight after a failed repetition is the critical responsibility of the spotter. The spotter must be quick to go to the lifter's aid if necessary. Usually, you will need one or two spotters; however, during a bench press or incline press, one spotter is sometimes preferable because it is easier to coordinate between a single spotter and a lifter than between two spotters and a lifter. You will need two spotters during a squat to stand on either side of the weight and assist in case the lift cannot be completed.

The lifter must communicate when the weight is to be removed. If the spotter steps in and removes the weight too early, the lifter may be deprived of completing the lift with additional effort. On the other hand, if there is too much delay in removing the weight, the lifter may suffer an injury.

CAUTION ▶   Because very heavy weights are sometimes used
during weight training exercises, spotters must
be wary of injuring themselves.

They must be in a good position to assist the lifter if needed, and they must observe the principles of proper lifting: bend the knees, maintain a straight back, and keep the weight close to the body (Figure 2–3).

Spotters are useful to help move a weight into position to begin an exercise. This activity again requires coordination between the spotters and the lifter, or the exercise will be much more difficult to complete. Signals should be worked out in advance so that everyone understands when the weight is to be raised from the rack. For example, the lifter may count "one, two, three" with the weight being lifted into position on "three." It is best to work with the same spotters on a regular basis because spotters and lifters learn what to expect from each other after working together for a while.

Figure 2–3 *Proper technique for spotting*

During the lift, spotters should be attentive, but should not disrupt the lifter's concentration. There is nothing worse than to be lifting and have a spotter so close that he or she makes you claustrophobic.

Spotters are also used to actively assist with the exercise. When doing negative exercises (eccentrics), the spotter may actually do most of the work for you during the positive (active phase) of the lift. Spotters can also provide additional force so that an exercise can be completed. Usually, this help amounts to a remarkably small change in effort. Lifters sometimes call this assistance the "magic fingers" because the spotter may be able to help complete a lift by lifting with just a couple of fingers.

Collars Collars secure weights to a barbell or dumbbell. It is quite common to see people lifting weights without collars, but to do so is dangerous. It is easy to lose your balance or to raise one side of the weight faster than the other. Without collars, the weights on one side of the bar will slip off, resulting in the weights on the opposite side crashing to the floor.

CAUTION ▶ Always be sure to use collars,
and make sure they secure properly.

Racks Racks are used to support weights in a position that is suitable for an exercise. Racks are designed for the bench press, incline press, squats, curls, and many other exercises. They should be sturdy and adjustable to different sizes so that they work for all lifters. In addition, they should also be accessible to spotters. Weights should be unloaded from the racks when not in use to prevent deterioration of the barbells.

Equipment Maintenance Most weight rooms are heavily used, so it is important that equipment is kept well maintained. Such equipment is safer and lasts longer. Collars and cables are particularly vulnerable to failure. With time, the threads on the collars become stripped making them useless and dangerous. They should be checked regularly and replaced or repaired as necessary. Cables on lat machines and wall pulleys become frayed with time and must be replaced. Serious injury may result if the cable snaps suddenly during an exercise. Weight trainers should report any equipment malfunction to the instructor immediately.

Equipment upholstery should be cleaned daily to prevent the spread of skin infections. Various manufacturers make cleaners that kill germs and protect the upholstery on weight machines and benches. Weight trainers can help maintain sanitary conditions by spreading a towel on upholstered equipment before using it.

Behavior in the Weight Room Weight trainers should always have the utmost respect for the equipment because misuse can result in a serious injury.

CAUTION ▶ Always be alert! There is no place
for horseplay in the weight room.

Medical Considerations While cautious weight training is reasonably safe, accidents do happen. Report any obvious injury to muscles or joints to the instructor or a physician. Don't keep working out in the hope that the injury will go away. Training with an injured joint or muscle can lead to a more serious injury.

Weight training tends to generate increased blood pressure that, although rare, can sometimes cause serious medical complications.

Report any headaches, chest, neck, or arm pains,   ◄ CAUTION
labored breathing, numbness, or visual disturbances
to the instructor immediately.

Consult a physician if you are unsure that weight training is an appropriate activity for you.

Proper Mechanics of Exercise

Each exercise has a proper technique. These techniques will be described in Chapters 3–7. There are several principles, however, that are common to all exercises. These principles will help you prevent injury and get the most from the weight training program.

Lifting Techniques Back injuries are among the most serious that can occur in the weight room. Most people have back pain at some time in their lives. Back pain can be prevented if basic principles of lifting are followed.

- ► Keep the weight as close to your body as possible. The farther out you hold a weight from your body, the more strain there is on your back.
- ► Do most of your lifting with your legs. The large muscles of the thighs and buttocks are much stronger than those of the back, which are better suited to maintaining an erect posture. Keep your hips and buttocks tucked in.
- ► When picking up a weight from the ground, keep your back straight and your head level or up. Bending at your waist with straight legs places tremendous strain on the lower back muscles and spinal disks.
- ► Do not twist your body while lifting. Twisting places an uneven load on back muscles, which causes strain.
- ► Lift the weight smoothly, not with a jerking, rapid motion. Sudden motions place more stress on the spinal muscles and disks.
- ► Allow for adequate rest between lifts. Fatigue is a prime cause of back strain.
- ► Lift within your capacity. Don't lift beyond the limits of your strength.

PROPER LIFTING TECHNIQUES

Poor lifting techniques are a common cause of many back injuries. To lift properly, follow these techniques:

▶ Keep your weight as close to your body as possible. The farther you hold a weight from your body, the more strain there is on your back.

▶ Do most of your lifting with your legs. The large muscles of the thighs and buttocks are much stronger than those of the back, which are better suited for maintaining an erect posture. Keep your hips and buttocks tucked in.

▶ When picking up an object from the ground, do not bend at your waist with straight legs because this action places tremendous strain on the low back muscles and disks.

▶ Do not twist while lifting. Twisting places an uneven load on back muscles, which can cause strain.

▶ Lift the weight smoothly, not with a jerking, rapid motion. Rapid motions place more stress on the spinal muscles.

▶ Allow adequate rest between lifts. Fatigue is a prominent cause of back strain.

▶ Lift within your capacity. Athletes should not lift a load beyond the limits of their strength.

Breathing Never hold your breath when you lift. Exhale when exerting the greatest force, and inhale when moving the weight into position for the active phase of the lift. Holding your breath causes a decrease in the volume of blood returning to the heart. Thus, blood cannot be pumped as easily to the brain. Holding your breath can cause you to become dizzy and, perhaps, to faint.

Exercise Movements Exercises should be performed smoothly and in good form. With practice, you will "groove" your lift, so that the weight is moved in the same general plane every time you do the exercise. In general, lower the weight relatively slowly and in control. Lift the weight forcefully during the active phase of the lift. Obviously, if you are using enough resistance, these powered movements will be relatively slow. However, you should attempt to perform the movements explosively. An old weight lifting saying to remember is to "go down slow and up fast."

Usually, you should not "bounce" the weights during the exercise. Bouncing means that you make an explosive transition between the pushing and recovery phase (that is, concentric and eccentric phases) of the lift. Bouncing is sometimes used by advanced weight trainers so that they can practice an exercise using heavier weight.

Never bounce a weight against the body.   ◄ CAUTION

While some experienced weight trainers use this training technique, it is not recommended because it can cause serious injury.

Perform all lifts through the full range of motion. Limiting the range of motion in exercises hampers flexibility and restricts strength gains within the range of motion practiced. "Muscle-boundness," which is often associated with weight-lifters, may be caused by not doing exercises through a full range of motion. Weight training does not inevitably lead to decreased flexibility. If you practice flexibility exercises and perform the weight training exercises properly, you can be both strong and flexible.

Grips Use the correct grip for each lift. There are three basic types of grip (Figure 2–4): pronated (palms away from you), supinated (palms toward you), and dead lift grips (one palm toward you, one away). The pronated grip is used in most presses, pulls, and squats. The supinated grip is used in exercises such as biceps curls and chin-ups. The dead lift grip is used in the dead lift exercise to increase your grip strength.

The thumbless grip and the thumblock grip are not recommended. The thumbless grip, as the name implies, involves placing the thumb in the same plane as the fingers. This grip, while placing the thumb under less stress, is dangerous because, for example, in a bench press you could easily lose control of the weight, and it could fall on you. The thumblock grip, in which the thumb is wedged between the index and middle fingers, places the thumb at increased risk of injury.

Figure 2–4 *Basic barbell grips: (a) pronated grip, (b) supinated grip, and (c) dead-lift or mixed grip*

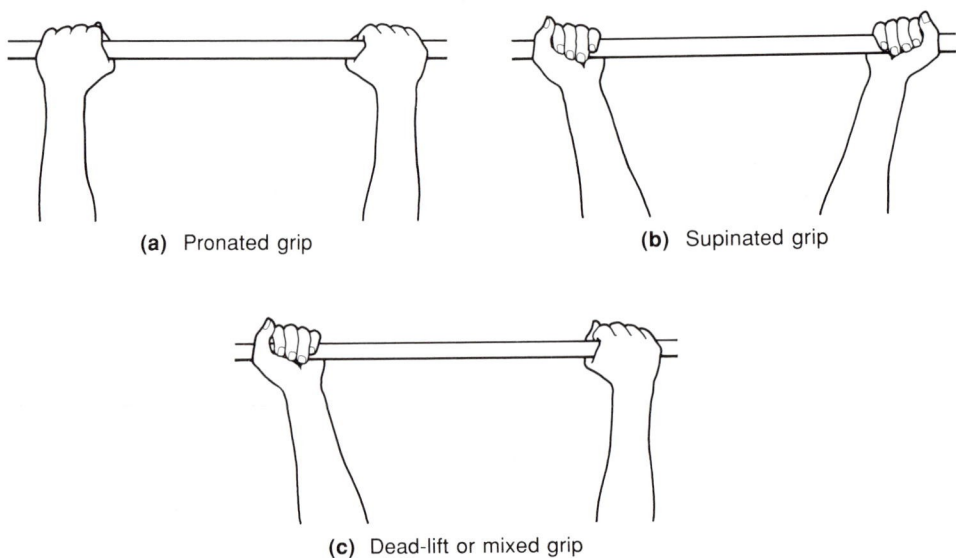

(a) Pronated grip

(b) Supinated grip

(c) Dead-lift or mixed grip

References

Arendt, E.A. Strength development: A comparison of resistive exercise techniques. *Contemp. Orthop.* 9:67–72, 1984.

Atha, J. Strengthening muscle. *Exercise and Sport Sciences Reviews* 9:1–73, 1981.

Berger, R. Optimum repetitions for the development of strength. *Research Quarterly* 33:334–338, 1962.

Fahey, T.D. (Ed.) *Athletic Training: Principles and Practice.* Mountain View, Ca.: Mayfield Publishing, 1986.

Fleck, S.J. and W.J. Kraemer. Resistance training: Physiological responses and adaptations. *Physician and Sports Med.* 16:108–124, 1988.

Garnica, R.A. Muscular power in young women after slow and fast isokinetic training. *J. Orthop. Sports Phys. Ther.* 8:1–9, 1986.

Hickson, R.C. Interference of strength development by simultaneously training for strength and endurance. *Eur. J. Appl. Physiol.* 45:255–263, 1980.

Jackson, A., T. Jackson, J. Hnatek, and J. West. Strength development: Using functional isometrics in an isotonic strength training program. *Res. Q. Exerc. Sport* 56:234–237, 1985.

Jacobson, B.H. A comparison of two progressive weight training techniques on knee extensor strength. *Athletic Training* 21:315–318, 1986.

Jenkins, W.L., M. Thackabery, and C. Killian. Speed-specific isokinetic training. *J. Orthop. Sports Phys. Ther.* 6:181–183, 1984.

Lesmes, G.R., D. Costill, E.F. Coyle, and W.J. Fink. Muscle strength and power changes during maximal isokinetic training. *Med. Sci. Sports* 10:266–269, 1978.

National Strength Coaches Association. Periodization. *NSCA Journal* 8:12–22, 1986.

Nelson, A.G., R.S. Chambers, C.M. McGown, and K.W. Pendrose. Proprioceptive neuromuscular facilitation versus weight training for enhancement of muscular strength and athletic performance. *J. Orthop. Sports Phys. Ther.* 7:250–253, 1986.

Noakes, T. *Lore of Running.* Cape Town, South Africa: Oxford University Press, 1985.

Nosse, L.J. and G.R. Hunter. Free weights: A review supporting their use in training and rehabilitation. *Athletic Training* 20:206–209, 1985.

O'Shea, P. Effects of selected weight training programs on the development of strength and muscle hypertrophy. *Research Quarterly* 37:95–102, 1964.

Osternig, L.R. Isokinetic dynamometry: Implications for muscle testing and rehabilitation. *Exerc. Sports Sci. Review* 14:45–80, 1986.

Verkhoshansky, U. How to set up a training program in speed–strength events (part 1). *Legkaya Atletika* 8:8–10, 1979. translated in: *Soviet Sports Review* 16:53–57, 1981.

Verkhoshansky, U. How to set up a training program in speed–strength events (part 2). *Legkaya Atletika* 8:8–10, 1979. translated in: *Soviet Sports Review* 16:123–126, 1981.

▼

CHAPTER THREE

Developing the **C**hest and **S**houlders

Chest and shoulder exercises are by far the most popular with people who train with weights. For women, these exercises improve the form of the chest and shoulders. For men, chest and shoulder exercises give them the T-shaped look of a powerful dynamo. Many sports require a strong upper body. Chest and shoulder exercises build a strength and power that helps men and women excel in the activities they enjoy.

Fortunes have been made on exercise devices that promised breast development in women. There is no exercise device that increases breast tissue. The breasts can, however, be made to look larger if the size of the chest muscles are increased. Because women have a limited ability to increase muscle size through weight training, they should not expect a fantastic increase in their chest measurement from such training.

The major muscles of the chest and shoulders are **multipennate**, which means that the muscle fibers are aligned in several directions. Because of this, you must perform a variety of exercises to work the muscles fully. For example, the pectoralis major muscle (the principle muscle of the chest), can be divided into upper, middle, and lower parts due to the different alignments of the fibers. Therefore, to fully train and develop this muscle, you must train each of the muscle's three segments differently. Likewise, the deltoid (the principle muscle of the shoulder) is a three-part muscle that requires three or more exercises to develop it fully.

It is extremely difficult to present exercises that functionally isolate specific muscle groups. For example, exercises for the chest, such as the bench press, also train the muscles of the arm, back, abdomen, and, to a limited extent, the legs (the legs stabilize the upper body in some chest and shoulder exercises). Throughout Chapters 3–7, exercises will be presented according to the body part they work the best.

EXERCISES TO BUILD THE CHEST

The pectoralis major is the principle muscle of the chest. It is functional in bringing the arm across the chest and lowering the arms when they are overhead. This muscle is essential to any movement that involves pushing. It is used during the forehand shot in tennis, when throwing a ball, blocking in football, and swimming freestyle.

The chief exercises for developing the chest include:

- ▶ Bench press
- ▶ Incline press
- ▶ Dumbbell flys
- ▶ Pullovers
- ▶ Decline press

Bench Press

The barbell bench press is probably the most popular weight training exercise. Most athletes gauge strength by the amount of weight a person can "bench." While the exercise is probably overemphasized, it provides strength and power that can be carried over to many sports and develops large and well-shaped muscles that look good. This exercise primarily develops the chest, the front of the shoulders, and the back of the arms.

▶ The Technique: Lying on a bench on your back with your feet on the floor, grasp the bar at shoulder width with your palms upward, away from your body (Figure 3–1). Lower the bar to your chest, and then return it to the starting position. The bar should follow an elliptical path, during which the weight moves from a low point at the chest to a high point over the eyes.

> During the motion, be careful not to arch your neck or   ◀ CAUTION
> back because this could result in injury to the spinal
> disks. Never bounce the weight off your chest because
> this could injure the ribs, sternum (breast bone), or
> internal organs.

You can also perform the bench press on many different weight machines.

It is best to use a bench with a built-in rack. The rack should be constructed so that the weight can be lifted on and off with little danger of pinching your hands. The rack and bench should be sturdy enough so that

Figure 3–1 *(a, b) Bench press. (c) Narrow-grip bench press places more stress on the triceps muscles.*

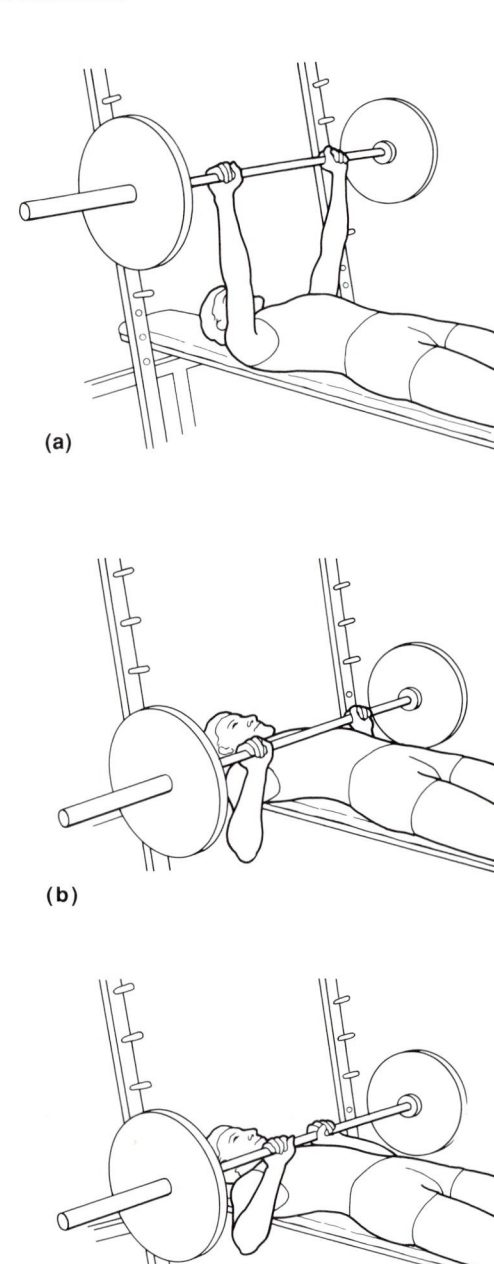

(a)

(b)

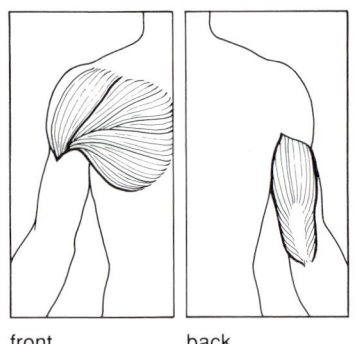

front   back

(c)

large weights can be supported safely. The bench should allow your arms and shoulders to travel freely during the exercise.

You can try emphasizing different muscle groups by varying the width of your grip. To increase the stress on the back of your upper arm (triceps muscle), narrow your grip; to stress the chest more, use a wider grip.

Variations of the Bench Press Several variations of this lift will help increase your bench press capacity or are good alternatives to it. These include the dumbbell bench press and the power rack bench press (Figures 3–2 and 3–3, respectively).

You will only be able to handle a fraction of the weight when using the dumbbell bench press compared to the barbell bench press. To perform the dumbbell bench press, begin by sitting on the bench with the dumbbells

Figure 3–2 *Dumbbell bench press*

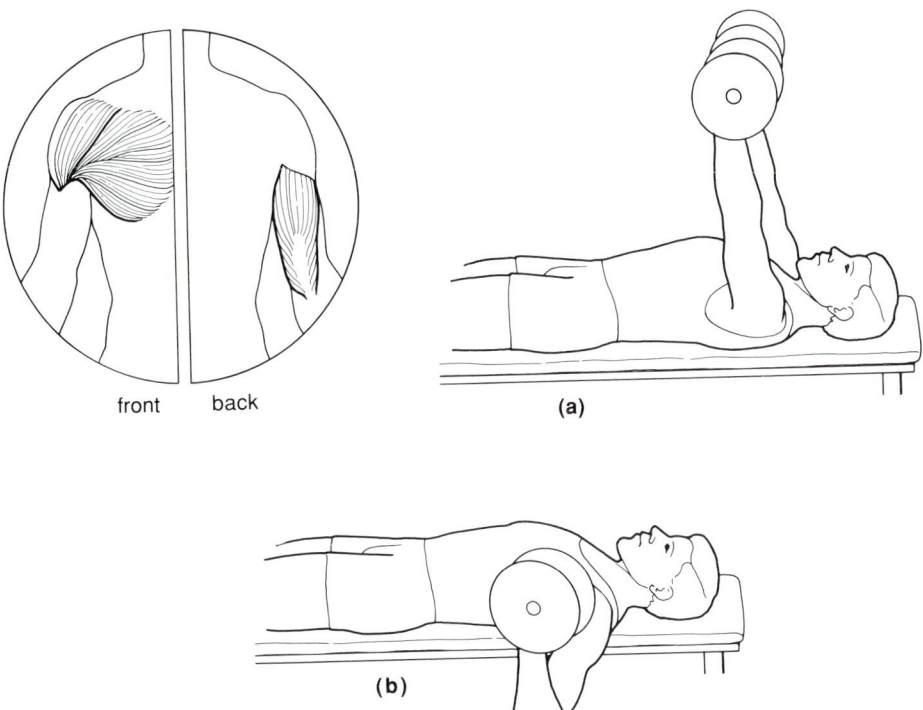

front   back

(a)

(b)

Figure 3-3 *Power rack bench press*

front   back

resting on your knees. Carefully rock backwards until your back is on the bench and the dumbbells are in your hands and resting on your chest. Push the dumbbells overhead until your elbows are extended, then return the dumbbells to your chest.

The power rack bench press is used to help overcome sticking points you may experience during the bench press. The power rack allows you to place pegs, or stops, at various points within the vertical range of motion. Place a bench inside the power rack and select three positions along the range of motion used during the exercise. The first pegs should be placed so that the bar can rest close to your chest. Lying in the basic bench press position with the bar resting on the first pegs, push the weight overhead. After you have completed your workout at the first level, move the pegs so that the bar rests in the middle of the range of motion. Repeat the exercise sequence. Finally, move the pegs so that the bar can only travel a few inches during the exercise. At this level, you will be capable of handling much more weight than you can normally bench press and is a safe way of getting used to increased weight.

A number of auxiliary exercises that will improve your bench press can be included in the training program. Incline presses, flys, and parallel bar dips with weights are described in the following sections.

Incline Press

The incline press is similar to the bench press except that the path of the bar is at a 45-degree angle to the plane of the chest rather than perpendicular to it. The exercise is performed while standing or sitting on a slant board. It develops the upper chest, the front of the shoulders, and the back of the arms and tends to give the chest a rounder appearance. Several equipment manufacturers make machines that simulate this lift.

▶ The Technique (Figure 3–4): Lying on an incline bench, grasp the bar at shoulder width and lower it to the upper part of your chest. Push the bar upward until your arms are extended. While pushing the weight, remember it is important to direct the bar upward toward the top of the head.

Pushing the weight too far in front of you will make ◀ CAUTION the exercise more difficult to perform and may result in a back, shoulder, or elbow injury.

Figure 3–4 *Incline bench press*

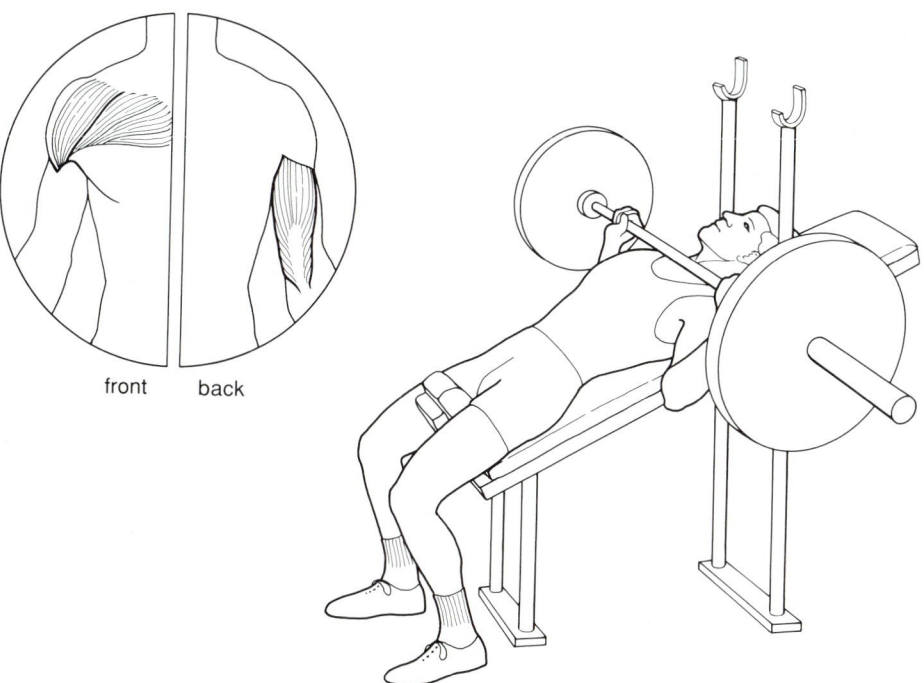

front   back

After pushing the weight overhead, lower it to the starting position. Don't lower the bar farther down your chest. You will need spotters on this lift in order to handle maximal loads. Racks will also help you use heavier weights and will make spotting safer and easier.

The incline press may be executed with a barbell or with dumbbells. Special skill is required to lift dumbbells to the starting position of the exercise. While sitting or standing on the incline bench (depending upon which type of bench you are using), grasp the dumbbells and place them on your knees. Beginning with the dumbbell in your left hand (if you are right handed), vigorously flex your knee upward, pushing the dumbbell into the starting position. Repeat this procedure with your other arm. After you have completed the exercise, slowly lower the dumbbells, either one at a time or both together, back to the floor.

Dumbbell Flys

Flys develop the chest and the front of the shoulders. They make use of dumbbells or machines that simulate the use of dumbbells. This exercise is good for developing the appearance of muscular fullness of the chest.

▶ The Technique (Figure 3–5): Lie back on a bench with a dumbbell in each hand, palms facing inward, and arms extended straight above your chest (starting position). Slowly lower the weights to the side until they reach shoulder level, then return them to the starting position. During subsequent training sessions, lower the weight to below shoulder level. Your arms can be straight or bent.

CAUTION ▶   Don't use too much weight when you first start doing
this exercise because there is a possibility of
injuring your elbows if the weight is excessive.

Begin with a weight that you can lift easily for at least ten repetitions, and increase the load gradually.

Pullovers

This is a good exercise for developing the pectoralis major, expanding the rib cage, and building the lats (latissimus dorsi, the large muscles of the back).

Figure 3–5 *Dumbbell flys: (a) bent arms, (b) straight arms*

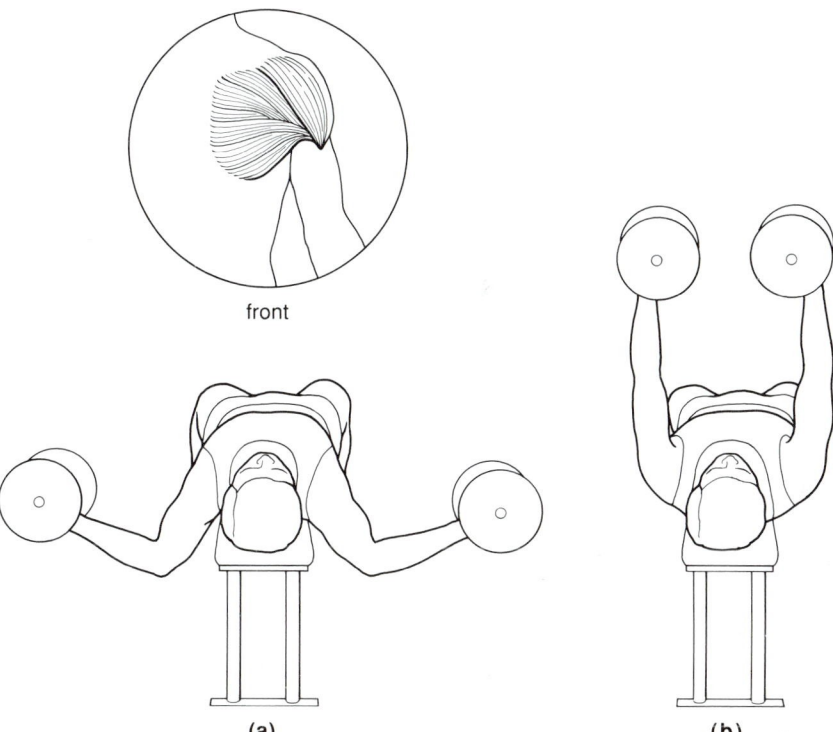

(a)   (b)

▶ The Technique: Lie on your back on the bench; your head should be raised slightly above the bench. Grasp a barbell with your hands about eight inches apart. With your arms bent slightly, lower the bar behind your head and reach toward the floor (Figure 3–6). Return the bar to the starting position, at rest in the middle of your chest. A single dumbbell can be used in place of the barbell. Generally, this exercise is accomplished with the bench placed perpendicular to the weight trainer (Figure 3–7). A variation to bent-arm pullovers is to use straight arms. Less weight should be used with straight arms to prevent elbow injury.

Decline Press

The decline press is not a usual part of the typical weight training routine. Used by body-builders to develop the lower part of the pectoralis major

Figure 3–6 *(a, b) Barbell bent-arm pullovers, (c, d) straight-arm pullover*

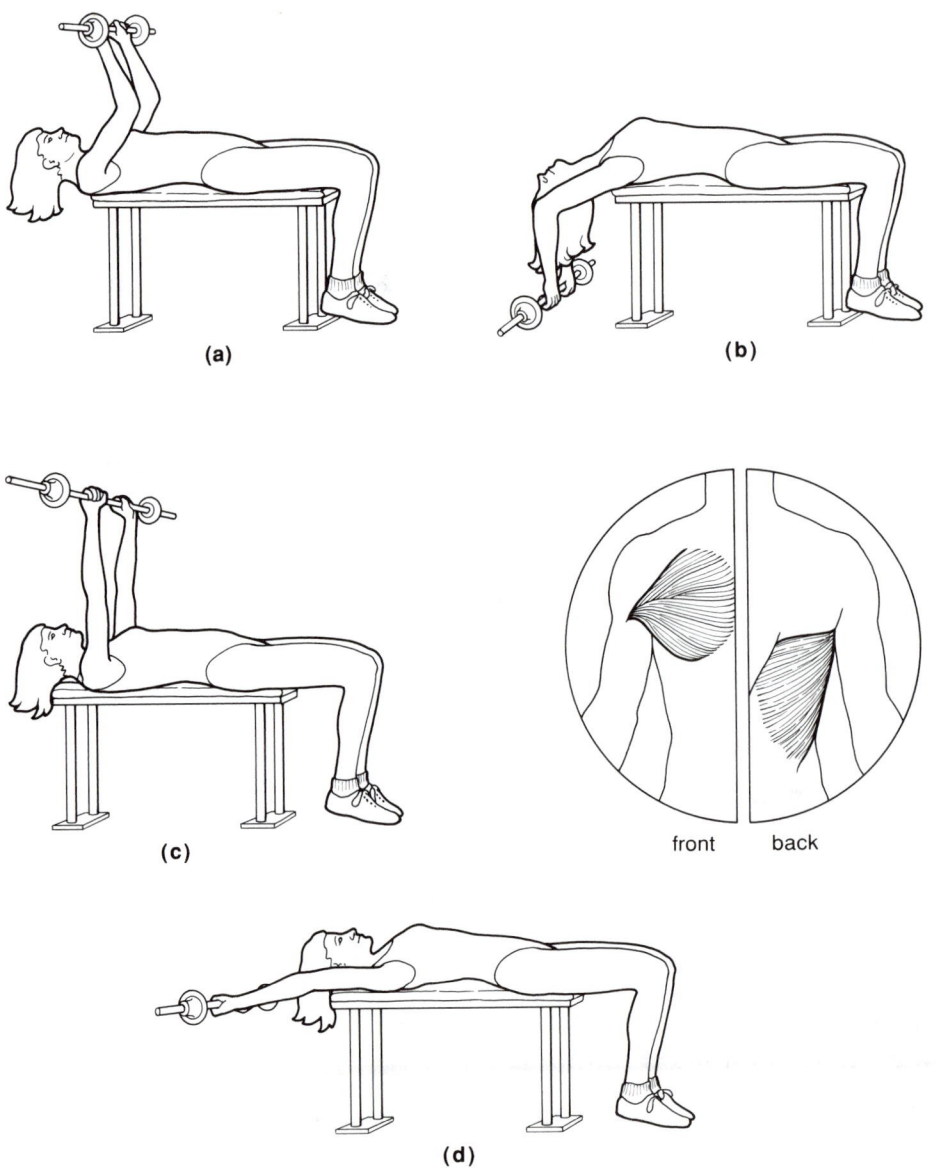

(a)

(b)

(c)

front   back

(d)

Figure 3–7 *Dumbbell pullovers*

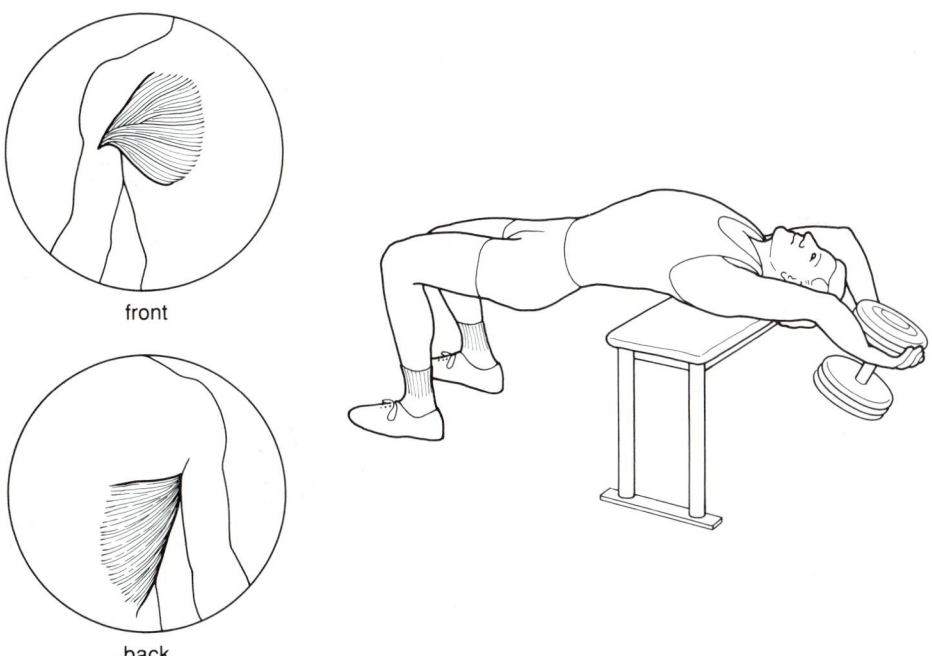

front

back

muscle, it also builds the front of the shoulders and the backs of the arms. It requires a specialized piece of equipment called a decline bench, which can be simulated by placing blocks under one end of a flat bench. Make sure the bench is steady and use spotters during this exercise. If you fail to complete this exercise, the weight could fall on your neck or face.

▶ The Technique (Figure 3–8): Lie on a decline bench, face up, with your head on the downward side. Grasp the weight at shoulder width, bring it to your chest, and then press it upward until elbows are extended. This exercise can also be done using dumbbells.

Additional Exercises for the Chest

Many other exercises develop the chest muscles to some extent including lat pulls, catching and throwing medicine balls, "crushers" (specialized

Figure 3–8 *Decline press*

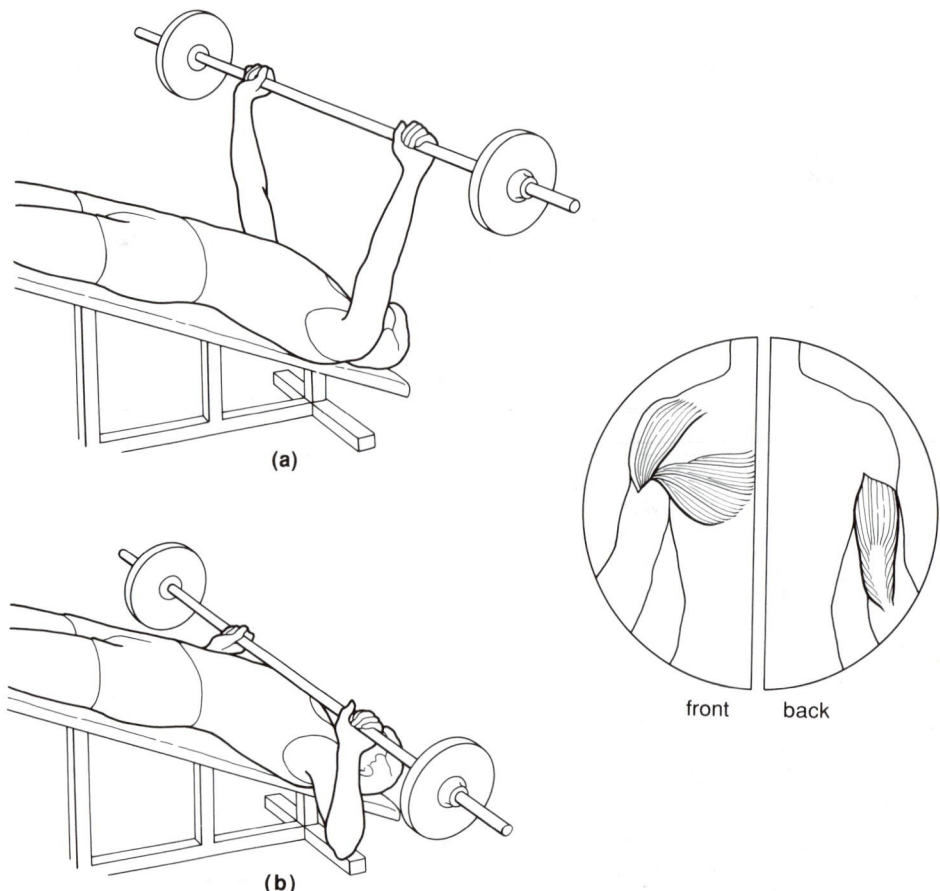

exercise devices that use movements resembling dumbbell flys), and horizontal push presses (in a standing position, push a weight horizontally as rapidly as possible). The old standby, the push-up, is a good chest exercise that doesn't require any equipment.

EXERCISES TO DEVELOP THE SHOULDERS

The shoulder is one of the most complex joints of the body, composed of six joints and more than 12 different muscles. The rest of this chapter focuses on the principle exercises that develop the shoulder's major muscle groups. In addition, exercises to train the "rotator cuff" muscles are described. The rotator cuff group, comprising four deep shoulder muscles, is important because it is often injured by swimmers and by softball, volleyball, and tennis players.

While all of the exercises described in the "chest" section of this chapter train the shoulder muscles also, the following exercises are generally recognized as being the best for developing the major muscles of the shoulder:

▶ Overhead press (shoulder press)
▶ Behind-the-neck press
▶ Raises
▶ Upright rowing

Overhead Press

The overhead press is also known as the military press and can be done standing or seated, with barbells or dumbbells.

Take care when standing not to arch the back excessively, or you may injure the spinal muscles, vertebrae (bones of the spine), or disks.   ◀ CAUTION

You should use a belt when performing unsupported overhead lifts such as overhead presses. This exercise develops the shoulders (deltoids), upper chest, and the back of the arms.

▶ The Technique: (1) The overhead press begins with the weight at your chest. A movement called the clean is used to raise the bar to the starting position (Figure 3–9). To perform the clean, place the bar on the floor in front of you. Keep your feet approximately two feet apart. Grasp the bar, palms down, with your hands spread to slightly more than shoulder width, and squat down, keeping your arms straight, your back at a 30-degree angle, and your head up. Pull the weight up past your knees to your chest while throwing your hips forward and shoulders back. Much of the power for the clean should come from your hips and legs. You can also use a rack to place the weights in the starting position. Ask your coach or weight training teacher to help you learn this lift because doing it improperly can lead to injury.

Figure 3–9 *The power clean is often used to move the bar into the starting position for the overhead press.*

Figure 3–10 *Standing press*

front   back

The overhead press (Figure 3–10): push the weight overhead until your arms are extended, then return to the starting position (weight at chest). *Again, when performing the press, be careful not to arch your back excessively*. Many equipment manufacturers have overhead press stations on their weight lifting machines.

Behind-the-Neck Press

A variation of the standing press is the behind-the-neck press. This exercise develops the shoulders, the back of the arms, and the upper back muscles. Avoid this exercise if you have a rotator cuff injury.

Figure 3–11 *(a) Press behind the neck—start; (b) press behind the neck—up*

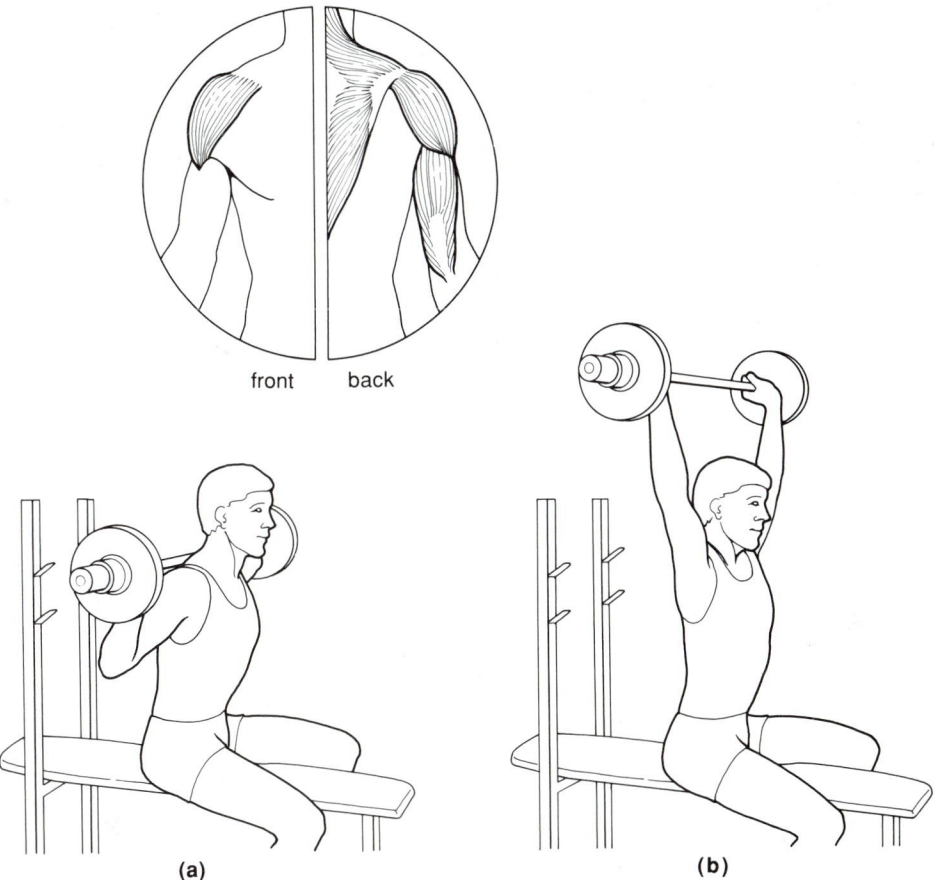

front   back

(a)   (b)

▶ The Technique (Figure 3–11): This exercise can be done standing or seated and requires a barbell. Use a rack to place the weight in the starting position. Using a fairly wide grip, place the weight behind your head and rest it on your shoulders. Push the weight above your head until your elbows are extended and then return to the starting position.

Raises

Raises are used to develop the deltoid muscle, a three-part, round muscle making up the most prominent part of the shoulder. This exercise must be done to the front, side, and rear to develop the deltoid fully. Lateral raises are usually done with dumbbells, although they can be done with wall pulleys or on specialized exercise machines.

▶ The Technique: Lateral raises (Figure 3–12): From a standing position, with a dumbbell in each hand and arms straight, lift the weights on both sides until they reach shoulder level, then return to the starting position. Bend your arms slightly if your elbows hurt. Some people continue the exercise until the weights meet overhead, but this is inadvisable as it may injure your shoulders. Side lateral raises develop the middle section of the deltoid muscle.

Figure 3–12 *Lateral raises*

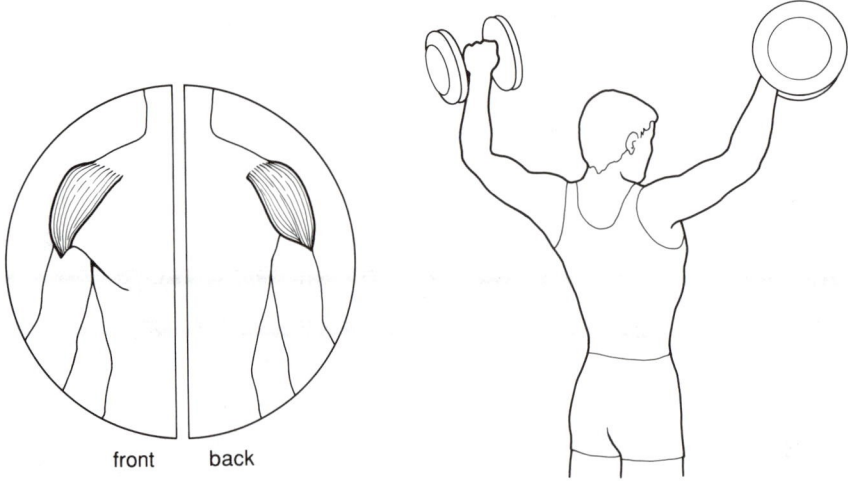

front   back

Figure 3–13 *Front raises*

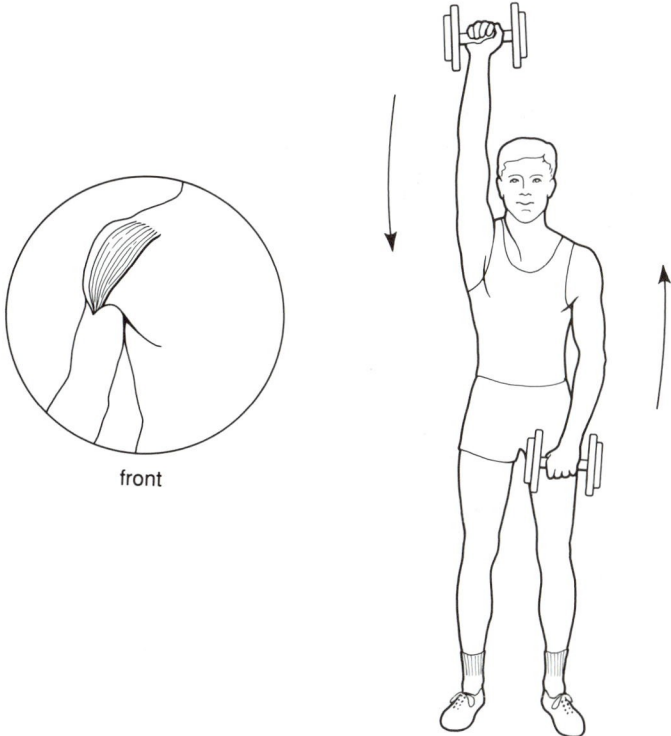

front

▶ The Technique: Front raises (Figure 3–13): From a standing position, using dumbbells or a barbell and with your arms straight, lift the bar in front of you to shoulder level, then return to the starting position. This exercise develops the front of the deltoid muscle.

▶ The Technique: Rear (bent-over) lateral raises (Figure 3–14): This exercise requires dumbbells. From a standing position, bend over forward with your back parallel to the floor and knees bent slightly. Lift the weights to both sides until they reach shoulder level, then return to the starting position. Bent-over lateral raises develop the back of the deltoids.

Upright Rowing

Upright rowing develops the shoulders, the front of the arms, the neck, and the upper back. Because it affects so many of the large muscle groups in the

Figure 3–14 *Bent-over lateral raises*

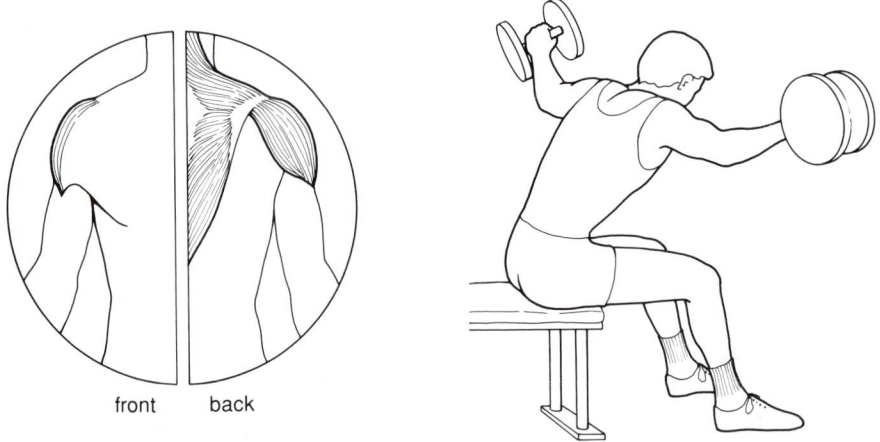

front   back

arms, shoulders, upper back, and neck at the same time, it is an excellent upper body exercise. This exercise can also be done with the body bent over forward. Although bent-over rowing also works the shoulders, it is a particularly good exercise for the upper back. (See Chapter 5.)

▶ The Technique: Using a pronated grip, grasp a barbell with your hands close together and stand with the weight at waist level (Figure 3–15). Pull the weight to the upper part of your chest, then return to the starting position.

Rotator Cuff Exercises

The rotator cuff of the shoulder is composed of four muscles that cause the humerus, the large bone of the upper arm, to rotate (turn) inward and outward. This muscle group is often injured in activities such as swimming, tennis, and throwing—exercises requiring the arm to go above shoulder level. The best way to prevent injuries to this muscle group is to make the muscles strong and flexible. Exercises to strengthen this muscle group include:

▶ Dumbbell external rotation
▶ Dumbbell internal rotation
▶ Empty can exercise

Figure 3–15 *Upright rowing*

front   back

Dumbbell External Rotation This exercise (Figure 3–16) strengthens muscles that rotate the arm outward (infraspinatus and teres minor). Lie on your side on a table, resting on one elbow. Bend your other elbow halfway (90 degrees), keeping the elbow tight to the rib cage. Slowly lower the weight, and then lift it back to the starting position.

Dumbbell Internal Rotation Lie on your back on a table with your elbow bent halfway (90 degrees) and held tightly against your side and with your hand extended over your chest (Figure 3–17). Slowly lower the weight to your side, and then slowly lift it back to the starting position.

Figure 3–16 *Exercise to strengthen shoulder external rotator muscles*

back

Figure 3–17 *Exercise to strengthen shoulder internal rotator muscles*

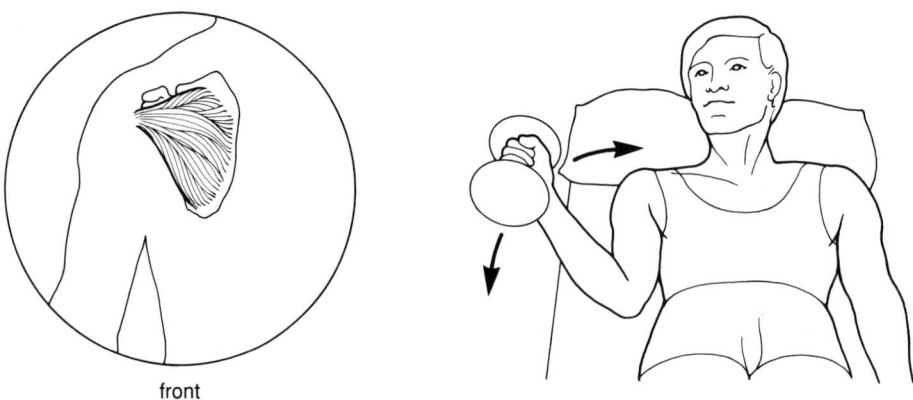

front

Empty Can Exercise This exercise (Figure 3–18) is probably the most important rotator cuff exercise because it strengthens the supraspinatus muscle, the muscle of the rotator cuff group that is injured most often in sports. Stand upright and hold a dumbbell in each hand. Keeping your arms straight, raise them to your shoulders, move them horizontally about 30 degrees, and rotate them inward as much as possible. Slowly lower and raise the weights through a 45 degree arc. The exercise got its name from the appearance that you are emptying liquid from two cans.

Figure 3–18 *Empty can exercise to strengthen the supraspinatus*

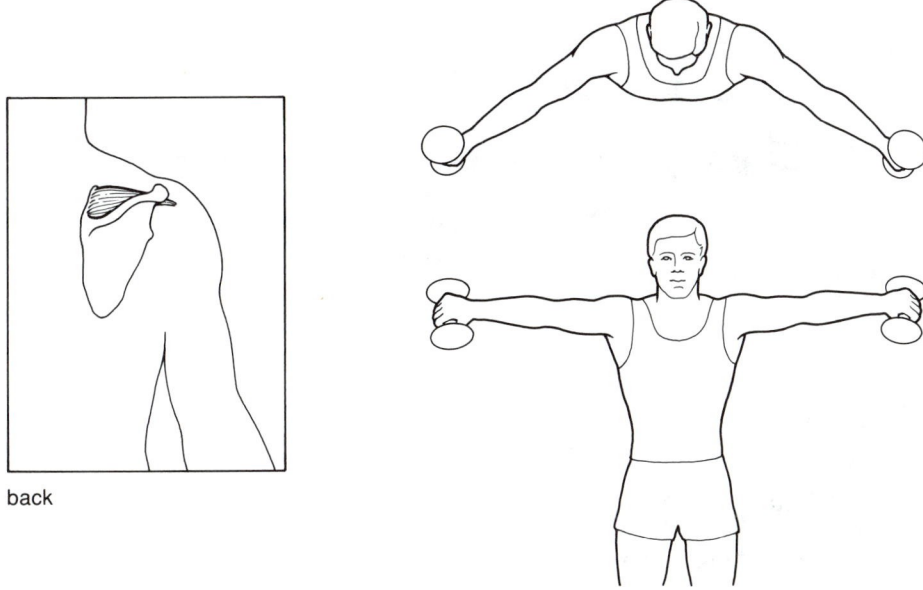

back

CHAPTER FOUR

▼

Exercises to Develop the Arms

We use our arms for almost every activity in work and play. Strong arms are helpful for such varied tasks as gardening, opening a can of peanut butter, throwing a ball, or hitting a tennis ball. While men generally prize large, well-defined arms, women usually value shapely arms. Strong, attractive arms are within the reach of anyone who is willing to devote a little time to developing them. This chapter presents basic arm and forearm exercises as well as specialized arm exercises for preventing "tennis elbow" and for increasing grip strength. For the sake of this discussion, exercises for the arms are divided into three categories: the front of the arm, the back of the arm, and the forearm.

EXERCISES TO DEVELOP THE FRONT OF THE ARM

Curls are the best exercises for developing the muscles of the front of the arm. The principle muscles of this area include the biceps brachius and the brachialis. Curls can be done using a barbell, dumbbells, or special curl bars. Curl bars (Figure 4–1) are useful because they reduce stress on the

Figure 4–1 *The curl bar*

forearm muscles, which allows you to use more weight and prevent injury to your forearms. There are many variations of curl exercises including:

- ▶ Standing barbell curls
- ▶ Dumbbell curls
- ▶ Preacher curls
- ▶ Reverse curls

Standing Barbell Curls

▶ The Technique: From a standing position (Figure 4–2), grasp the bar with your palms upward, your hands shoulder width apart. Keeping your

Figure 4–2 *Standing barbell curl*

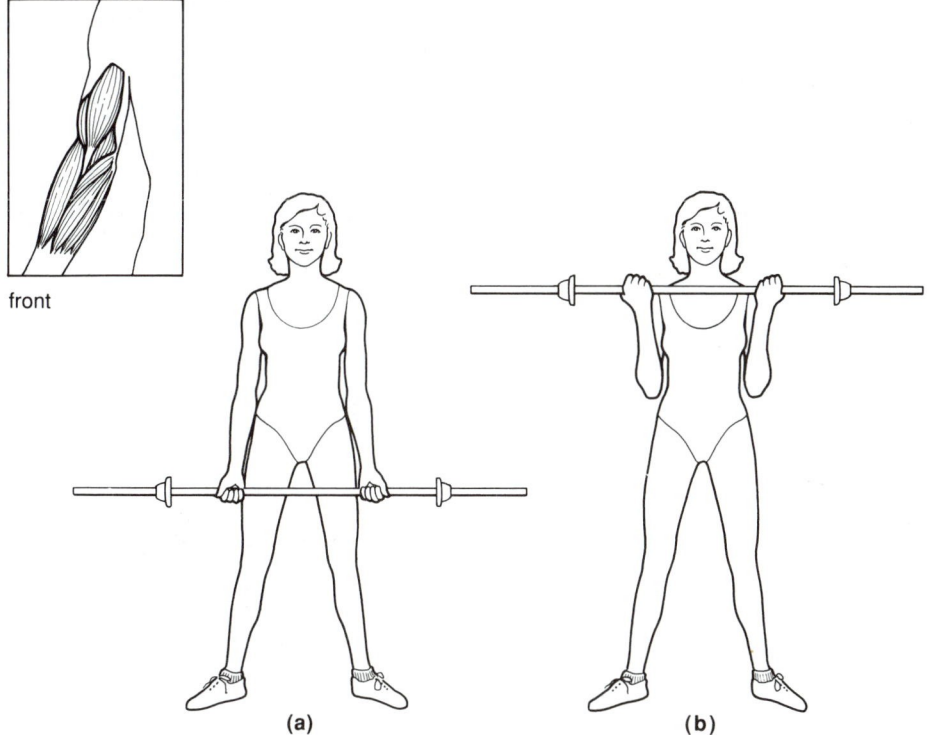

front

(a)   (b)

upper body rigid, bend (flex) your elbows until the bar reaches a level slightly below the collarbone. Return the bar to the starting position.

CAUTION ▶   Be sure not to arch your back during this exercise,
                   or injury may result. If you are using heavy weights,
                   it is a good idea to use a weight lifting belt.

Dumbbell Curls

There are many ways of doing dumbbell curls—seated on a flat bench, seated on an incline bench, alternating between arms, doing both arms at the same time, and doing all the repetitions with one arm before doing them for the other arm. While there is little difference between these lifts, each lift stresses the arm in a slightly different way and can be substituted for another occasionally to add variety to the program.

▶ The Technique: While seated on a flat or incline bench (Figure 4–3), grasp the dumbbells using a supine grip (palms up). Begin with the arms

Figure 4–3 *Seated dumbbell curl*

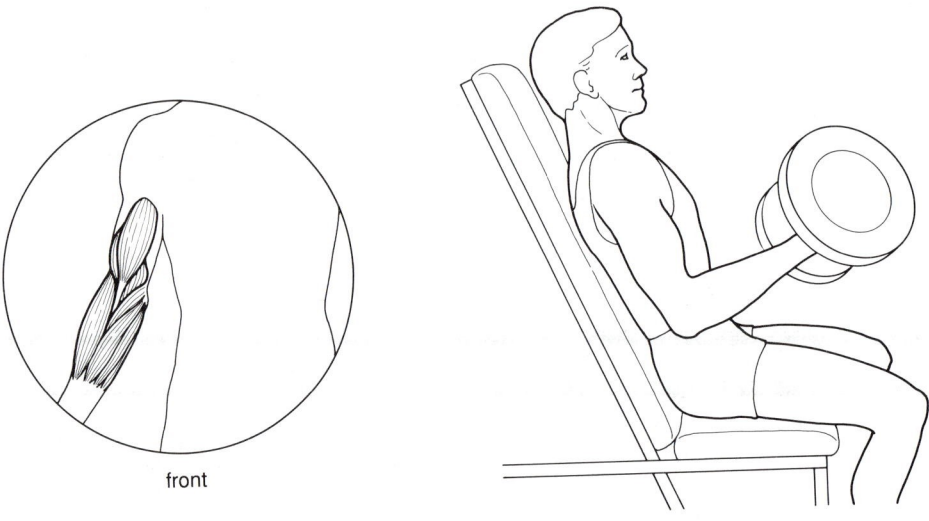

front

extended, and bend the arms until the weights approach your shoulders, then return to the starting position. Swinging the weights or bending your back while doing dumbbell curls will make the exercise less effective.

Preacher Curls

Preacher curls is an exercise that effectively isolates the muscles of the front of the arm. It is extremely difficult to cheat in this lift; consequently, the lift is very effective in building up the biceps. It requires a special apparatus called a preacher stand, so named because it resembles a pulpit, If a preacher stand is not available, an incline bench can be substituted. Some equipment manufacturers produce weight machines that simulate this lift.

▶ The Technique (Figure 4–4): This lift can be accomplished using a barbell, dumbbells, or curl bar. Using a supinated grip, place your elbows on the preacher stand and fully extent your elbows. Bend your arms (curl

Figure 4–4 *Preacher curls using preacher stand*

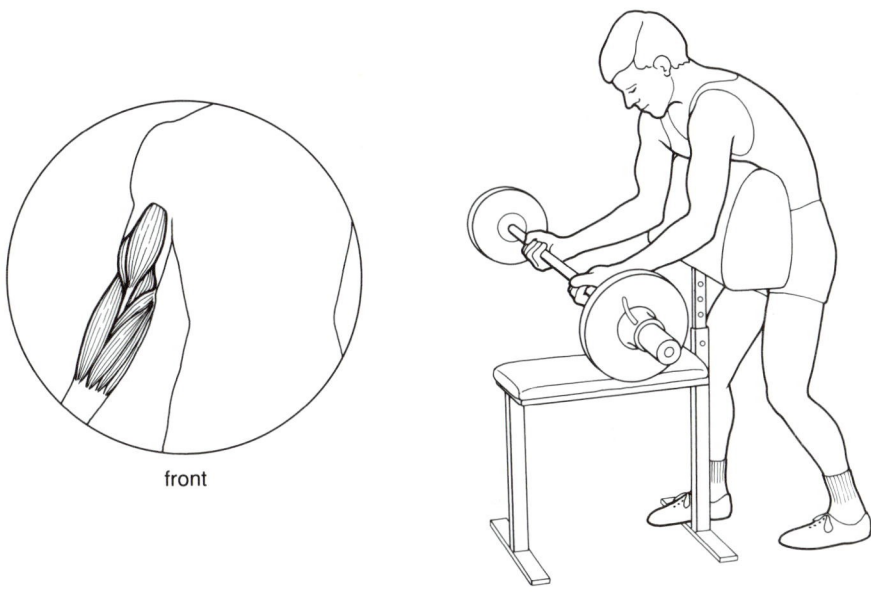

front

the weight) until they almost reach your collarbone, then return to the starting position.

Reverse Curls

Reverse curls have a similar effect to the curls, except they place a different stress on the forearm muscles. This exercise can be done with a barbell, dumbbell, or curl bar in a seated or standing position.

▶ The Technique (Figure 4–5): Stand holding the weight at your waist, using a pronated grip (palms down, opposite of curls described previously). Lift the weight by bending at your elbows until the bar almost reaches your collarbone, then return to the starting position.

Figure 4–5 *Reverse curls (note grip)*

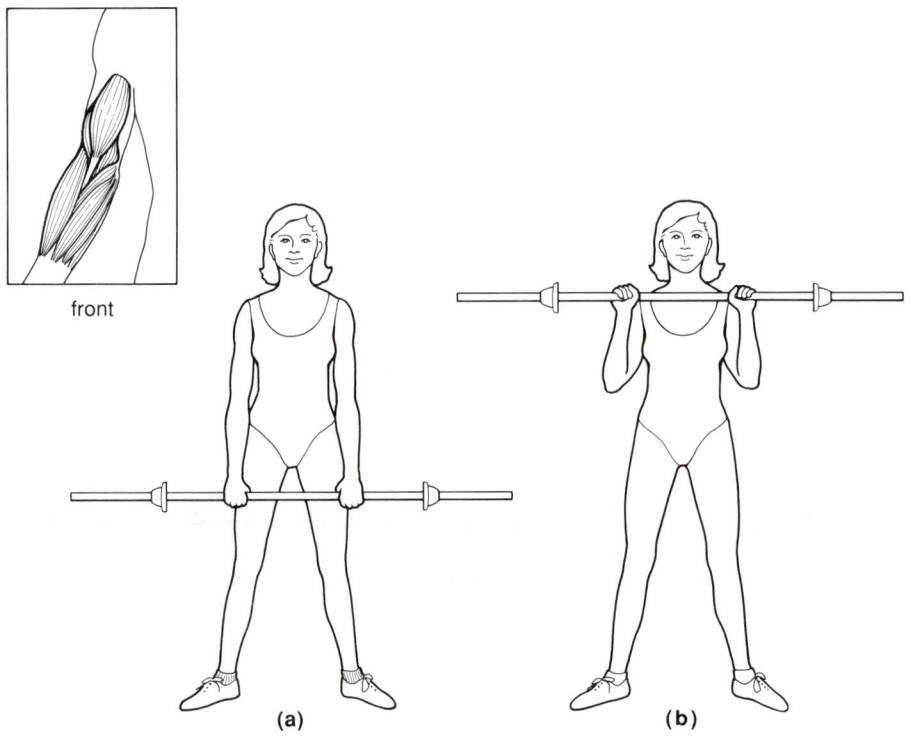

front

(a)   (b)

Other Exercises for the Front of the Arm

Any exercise that stresses your arm muscles as you bend your elbow will work this part of your body. Exercises that work the biceps as well as the muscles of other joints include pull-ups, chin-ups, lat pulls, and rowing exercises.

EXERCISES TO DEVELOP THE BACK OF THE ARM

The triceps is the major muscle of the back of the arm and is trained during all pressing exercises. Examples of exercises that are particularly good for building the triceps are:

▶ Triceps pull-downs on the lat machine
▶ French curls
▶ Bench triceps extensions
▶ Parallel bar dips

Triceps Pull-Downs on the Lat Machine

In general, exercises that require expensive gym equipment are not included in this book. However, because a lat machine is found in most weight rooms, a description is necessary. The triceps pull-down is an excellent exercise for isolating the triceps muscles. If you develop elbow pain as a result of doing this exercise, try another of the triceps exercises listed previously and discussed in the following sections.

▶ The Technique: Using a narrow, pronated grip, grasp the bar of the lat machine and fully extend your arms (Figure 4–6) with your elbows held closely at your side (starting position). With elbows locked to your side, allow your hands to be pulled up to your chest, then firmly push the weight back to the starting position. If your elbows move during this exercise, you are cheating.

Figure 4–6 *Triceps pushdowns*

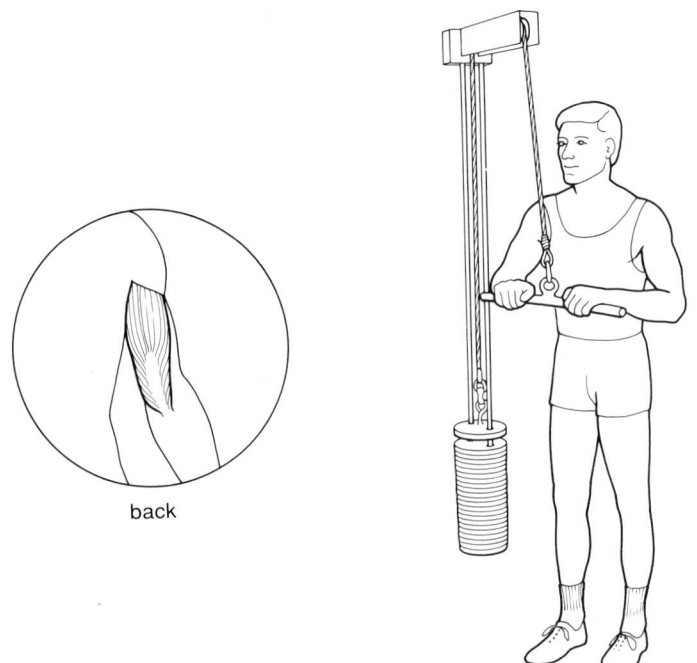

back

Figure 4–7 *French curls (seated triceps extensions)*

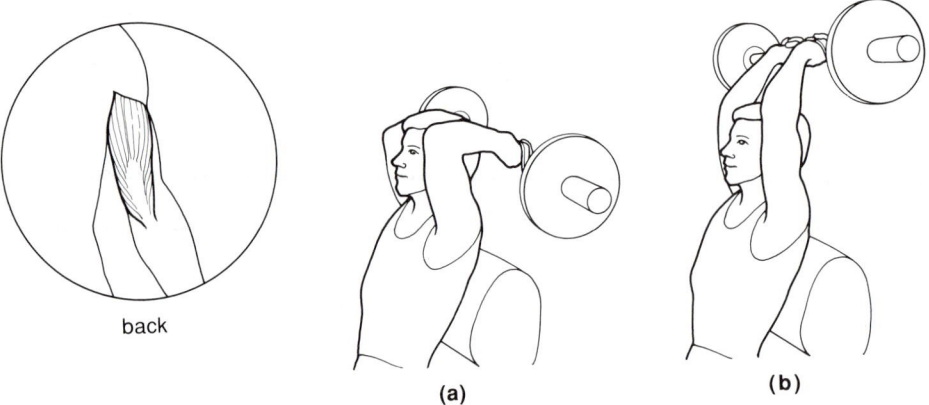

back

(a) (b)

French Curls

This exercise appears to be similar to the behind-the-neck press, but if done properly, it is very effective in isolating the triceps. The basic difference between the two exercises is that the behind-the-neck press involves movement of the shoulder and elbow joints, while in French curls the shoulders are fixed and the movement occurs in the elbow joints.

▶ The Technique: Grasp a barbell behind your head, using a pronated grip with your hands approximately 6–12 inches apart (Figure 4–7). Keeping your elbows up and stationary, extend your arms until the weight is overhead, then return to the starting position.

Bench Triceps Extension

This exercise is similar to French curls.

Be careful not to use too much weight because, if you ◀ CAUTION
lose control of the bar during the exercise, a serious
head injury could result.

▶ The Technique: Lie on a bench, grasping a barbell with a pronated grip with your hands 6–12 inches apart (Figure 4–8). Push the weight above

Figure 4–8 *Bench triceps extension*

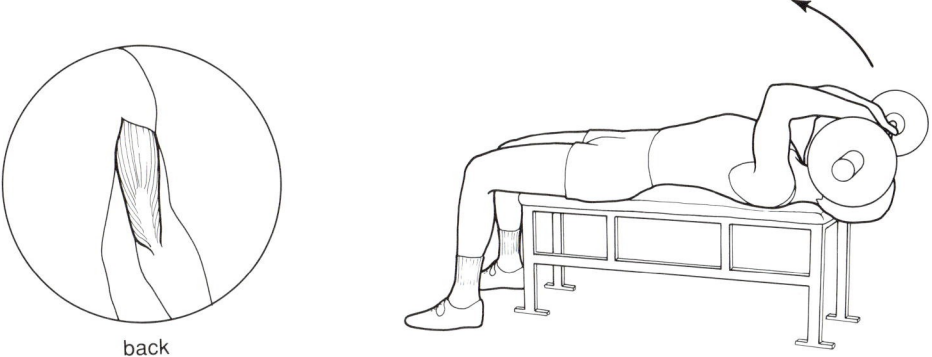

back

your chest until your elbows are extended (starting position). Keeping your elbows in a fixed position, carefully lower the weight until it touches your forehead, then push the weight back to the starting position.

Parallel Bar Dips

This exercise is excellent for improving your bench press as well as for building your triceps. As your strength improves, you can make the exercise more effective by placing a rope or chain through your weight belt and suspending weights from it. The rope or chain should have a fastener, so there is no danger of the weights falling during the exercise.

▶ The Technique: Support yourself between the parallel bars (Figure 4–9) on your fully extended elbows. Lower yourself slowly by bending your elbows until your chest is almost level with the bars. Then push up until you reach the starting position.

Figure 4–9 *Parallel bar dips*

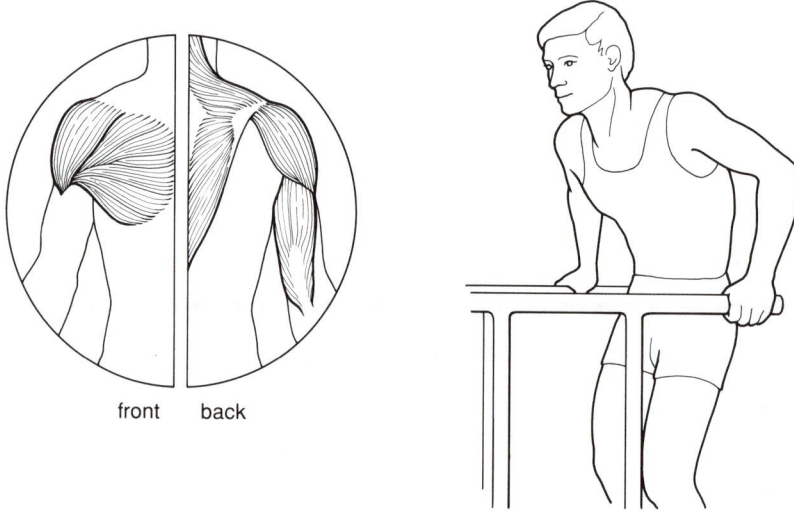

front   back

EXERCISES TO DEVELOP THE FOREARM MUSCLES

Forearm muscles are essential to any activity requiring that you rapidly snap your wrist such as in golf, the tennis serve, badminton, and in throwing a ball. Weakness of the forearm muscles results in a condition called tennis or carpenter's elbow. Forearm muscles are also largely responsible for grip strength. Exercises that develop the forearm muscles include wrist curls and wrist rollers.

Wrist Curls

Wrist curls are done using either a pronated or supinated grip. Pronated or reverse wrist curls build the wrist extensors, the muscles injured in tennis elbow. Supinated wrist curls build the forearm flexors and are important auxiliary exercises to biceps curls.

▶ The Technique: This exercise can be done with either a barbell or dumbbells (Figure 4–10). In a seated position, with forearms resting on your thigh and hands extending over the edge of your knees, use a supinated grip to lower the weight as far as possible, then lift your hands upward by bending at the wrists as much as possible. Repeat this exercise using a pronated grip.

Lateral wrist curls are a variation of wrist curls. This exercise requires the use of a small bar with the weight affixed at one end. Perform the exercise in the same manner as for wrist curls, except bend your wrist laterally (to the side).

Wrist Rollers

This exercise requires a machine (such as can be found on the Universal Gym) or a wrist roller device. The wrist roller device can be purchased or constructed from a cylindrical piece of wood with a hole drilled through it which then is tied to a three foot length of rope or small chain. The weight is attached to the other end of the rope.

▶ The Technique: While holding the piece of wood straight out in front of you with both hands (Figure 4–11) use a pronated grip to lift the weight by winding the rope around the wood.

Figure 4–10 *Wrist curls: (a) extension, (b) flexion, and (c) using two dumbbells at once*

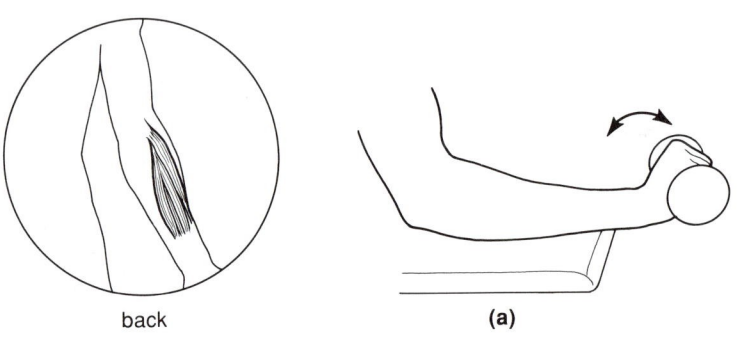

back   **(a)**

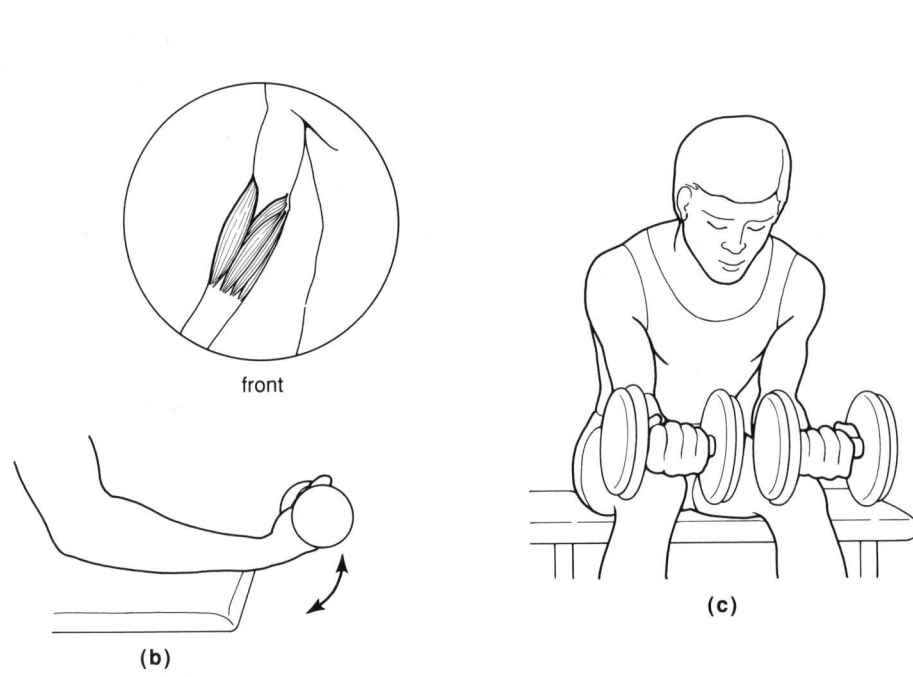

front

(b)

(c)

Figure 4–11 *Wrist rollers*

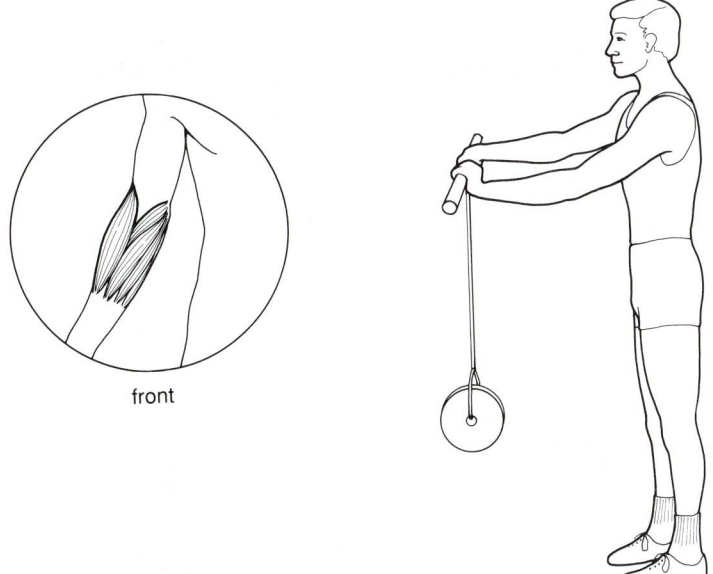

front

Additional Exercises for the Forearms and Grip

Most competitive weight-lifters and elite weight-trained athletes, such as discus throwers and professional football players, have amazingly strong forearms and grips, yet few of them do wrist rollers or wrist curls. Large-muscle weight lifts, such as cleans, snatches, and dead-lifts, place considerable stress on the forearms and hands. If you do those lifts, you will also develop a good grip and strong forearms.

If you don't want to do pulling exercises, carry around a small rubber ball and squeeze it inside your fist every time you think about it. This exercise is very effective for developing grip and forearm strength.

▼

CHAPTER FIVE

Exercises for the Neck and Back

Most people have trouble with their neck and back during their lifetime, yet this part of the body is often neglected by weight trainers. The spine is composed of a series of bones called vertebrae, with the spinal cord running through a channel in these bones. Between each vertebra lie shock absorbers called intervertebral disks. The spine has three natural curves that aid the disks in absorbing shock, and strong muscles are important for maintaining these curves.

The disks are subject to injury when exposed to excessive forces. Weight trainers must take special care to select exercises that do not damage the intervertebral disks. Nerves emanate from the spinal cord and act as messengers between the tissues and the central nervous system. Pain and muscle spasm result if abnormal pressure is put on these nerves. Strong neck and back muscles help maintain the proper alignment of the vertebrae and prevent pressure on the spinal nerves.

Strong neck and back muscles are critical for movement in humans. Because the neck controls the movement of the head, strong neck muscles are important in any sport. The middle and upper back muscles are also vital in almost all movements and provide a balance to the muscles of the front of the body. The lower back muscles help maintain the body in an upright posture and are important in bending movements. Because the lower back is notoriously vulnerable to injury, it is necessary to keep these muscles strong and flexible.

The following discussion is divided into exercises for the neck, upper back, and lower back. There is, however, considerable overlap between these areas, and exercises described in other parts of the book often affect the neck and back.

EXERCISES FOR THE NECK

Strong neck muscles are important to all active people, particularly those involved in football, wrestling, gymnastics, diving, the throwing events in track and field, and rugby. Most people do not follow a systematic program for strengthening the neck muscles even though the neck is vulnerable to serious injury. Neck pain affects many people, and the cause is often poor strength in the neck and in upper back muscles.

Including basic neck strengthening   ◀ CAUTION
exercises in the weight training
program will help prevent neck injuries.

The intensity of neck exercise should be increased gradually, particularly if you are recovering from a neck injury or suffer from neck pain. Neck muscles are relatively small and are thus more susceptible than larger muscle groups to the destructive effects of sudden overload.

There are three basic techniques for strengthening the neck:

▶ Manual resistance exercises

▶ Neck harness exercises

▶ Neck machine exercises

Manual Exercise

Manual resisted neck exercises provide an exercise load in all neck motions. Manual exercise is an easy, inexpensive way to strengthen neck muscles and can be incorporated almost anywhere in the program. For example, it can be added to your stretching routine prior to running or included as one of your weight training exercises.

Caution is essential: Manual resistance can be   ◀ CAUTION
very dangerous if excessive force is used.

Have your coach instruct you in proper technique before attempting these exercises.

▶ The Technique: Do these exercises on only one side of the body at a time. Do not cross the body's midline. Three movements should be used in your manual resistance neck training program: flexion, extension, and lateral flexion.

Manual neck flexion (Figure 5–1): Lie on your back on a table with your head hanging over the edge. Have your training partner supply resistance to your forehead as you attempt to bring your chin to your chest. Resistance should be minimal when you first start doing this exercise.

Manual neck extension (Figure 5–2): Lie on your stomach on a bench with your head hanging over the edge. Have your training partner supply resistance to the back of your head as you attempt to bring it toward the back of your spine.

Figure 5–1 *Manual neck flexion*

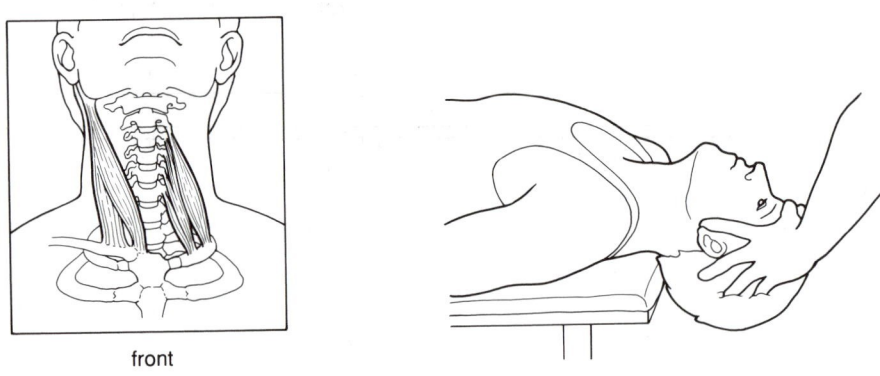

front

Figure 5–2 *Manual neck extension*

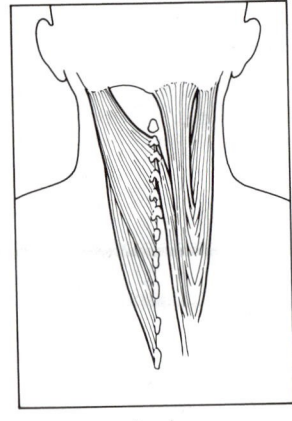
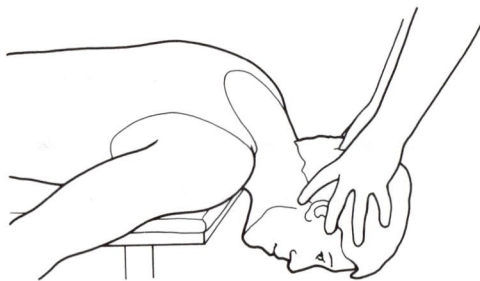

back

Figure 5–3 *Manual neck lateral flexion*

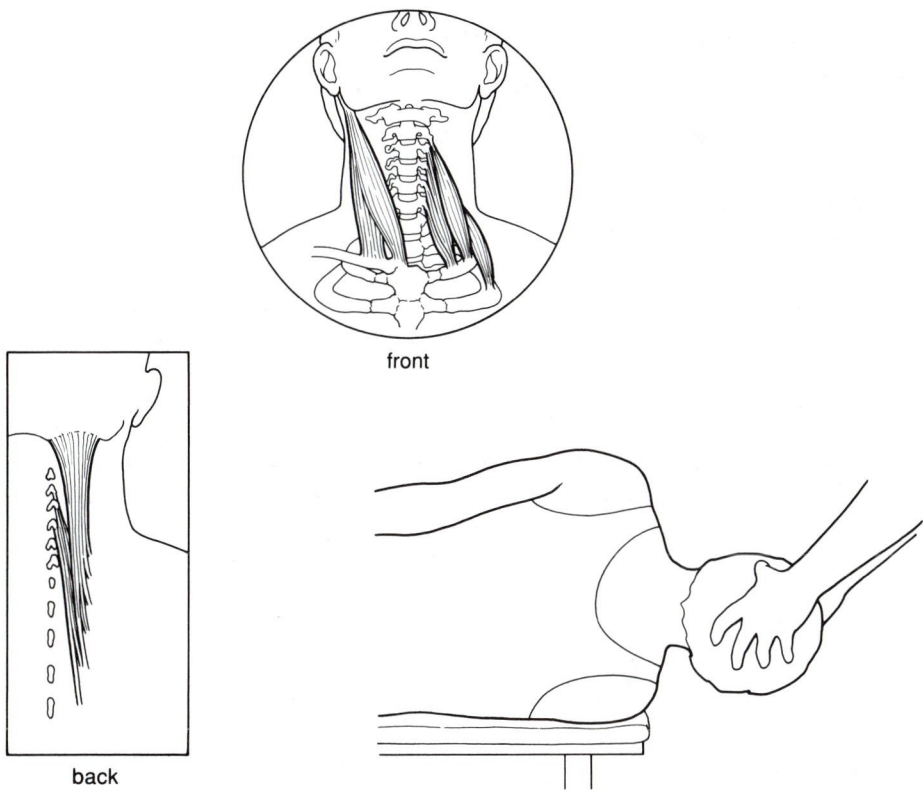

front

back

Manual neck lateral flexion (Figure 5–3): Lie on your side on a table with your head hanging over the edge. Have your training partner supply resistance to the side of your head as you attempt to bring your ear up to your shoulder. Do this exercise on the right and left sides of your body.

You can provide manual resistance to yourself by pushing on the front, back, or side of your head as you perform the various neck movements.

Neck Harness Exercises

Neck harness exercises involve the same movements as manual resistance neck exercises except that resistance is provided by weights suspended from a neck harness rather than by a training partner. Neck harnesses are relatively inexpensive and can be purchased at almost any sporting goods store.

▶ The Technique: The neck harness can provide resistance to the neck during neck flexion, extension, and lateral flexion.

Neck extension (Figure 5–4): Wearing the neck harness with the weight suspended from the harness chain, stand with your knees bent and hands on your thighs. Slowly lower the weight with your neck as far as possible, then return to the starting position.

Neck flexion (Figure 5–5): Wearing the neck harness with weight suspended from the harness chain, lie on your back on a table. Allow your head to slowly roll backward, then pull the weight back up by moving your chin toward your chest. Make sure to hold the sides of the table with your hands so you don't lose your balance.

Neck lateral flexion (Figure 5–6): Wearing the neck harness with weight suspended from the harness chain, lie on your side on a table. Allow your head to slowly bend to the lower side, then pull the weight upward by moving your ear toward your higher shoulder. Do this exercise on the right and left sides of your body.

Neck Machine Exercises

A number of equipment manufacturers make neck exercise machines that provide resistance during neck flexion, extension, lateral flexion, and rotation. If you have access to this equipment, try to use it because it is probably superior to performing the manual or neck harness methods.

Figure 5–4 *Neck flexion with harness*

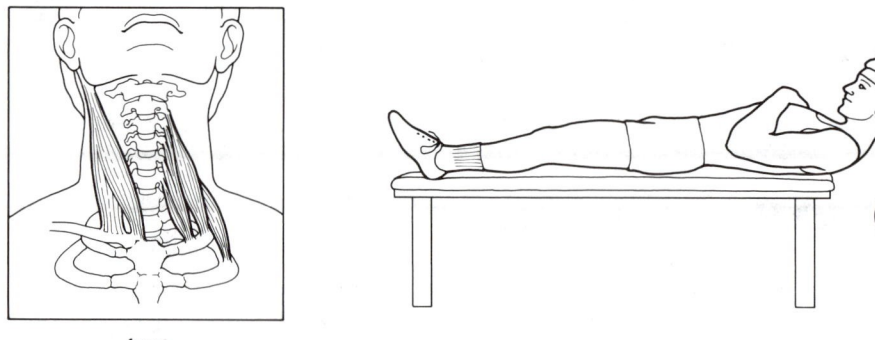

front

Figure 5–5 *Neck extension with harness*

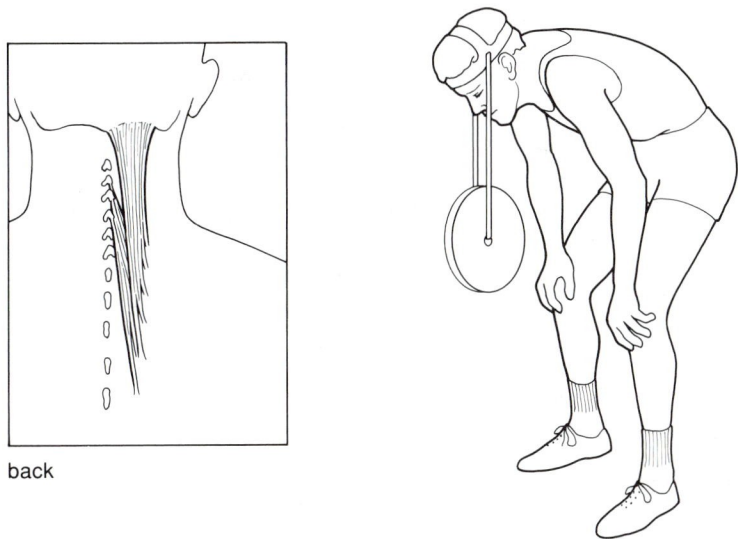

back

Figure 5–6 *Neck extensions on neck machine*

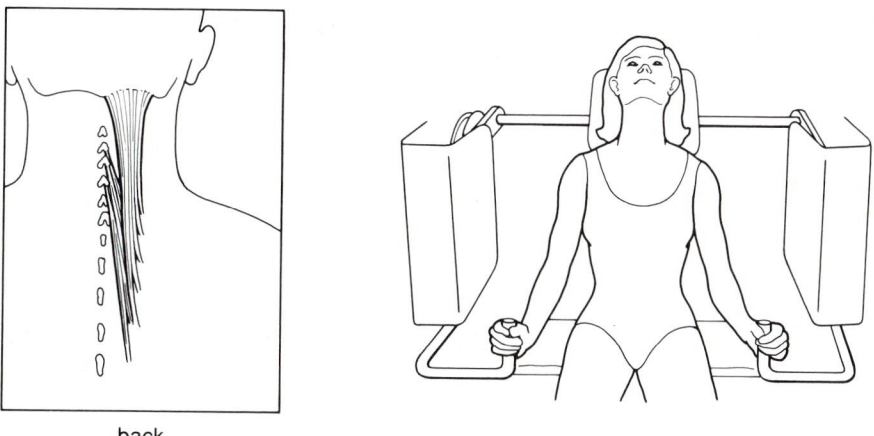

back

Neck Bridges

Neck bridges are popular among football players and wrestlers. This exercise involves being in contact with the ground with both your head and feet. Thus, body weight is supported mainly by the neck muscles. Never do neck bridges when recuperating from an injury because they may subject recovering muscles to an intolerable overload. Although neck bridges are an acceptable part of the neck injury prevention program for healthy athletes, they should be practiced with the other exercises discussed in this chapter to develop maximum strength and muscle endurance in the neck. Some sports medicine experts feel that no one should practice neck bridges. Certainly, this exercise should not be practiced until your neck is strong enough to handle it.

EXERCISES TO DEVELOP THE UPPER BACK

In the upper back the two chief muscles important for human movement are the trapezius and latissimus dorsi. These muscles are known to most weight trainers as the "traps" and "lats." Many exercises presented in this book develop the upper back.

Trapezius (Trap) Exercises

Two exercises that are good for specifically training the traps are shoulder shrugs and rowing exercises. The traps are also developed when you do overhead presses (see Chapter 3) and pulling exercises (cleans, snatches, and high pulls; see Chapter 7). If you are doing overhead presses and pulling exercises, you probably don't need to do additional exercise for this muscle.

Shoulder Shrugs Shoulder shrugs can be done with a barbell or with commercially manufactured shoulder shrug machines. It is easy to cheat on this exercise by letting your legs initiate the movement, so it is important to use the trapezius to do the work.

▶ The Technique: Using a barbell and a pronated grip, stand, holding the weight at shoulder width with arms extended and the weight resting

Figure 5–7 *Shoulder shrugs*

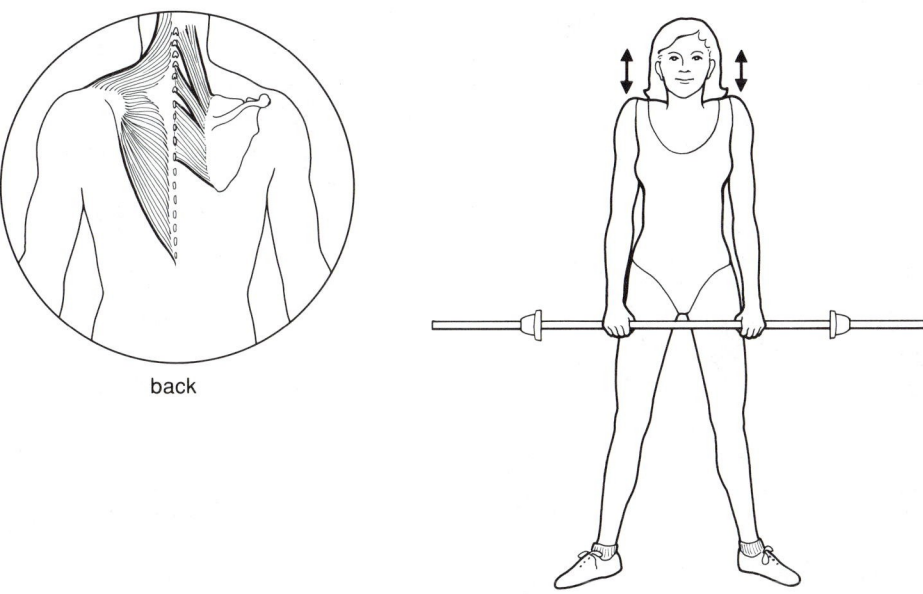

back

below your waist (Figure 5–7). Without unlocking your elbows, shrug your shoulders up toward your head, then return to the starting position.

Bent-over Rowing Upright rowing is described in Chapter 3 as a good shoulder exercise. In addition to working the major muscles of the upper back, bent-over rowing also works the shoulders.

▶ The Technique: Bend over at the waist with your knees bent and arms extended, holding a barbell (Figure 5–8). Lift the weight to your chest, then return to the starting position. This exercise may place excessive pressure on your intervertebral disks, so it should be avoided if you have back trouble.

Latissimus Dorsi (Lat) Exercises

Big lats give a V-shape to the back. These muscles are extremely important in many types of physical activity because they pull the arms downward,

Figure 5–8 *Bent-over rowing*

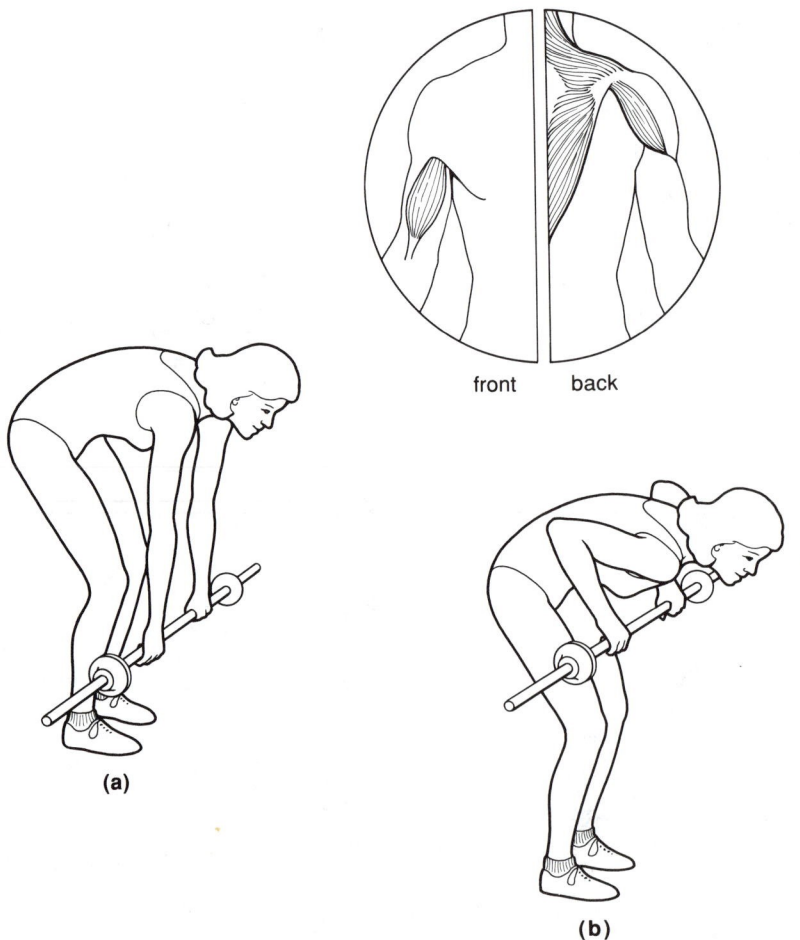

front   back

(a)

(b)

backward, and inward. A variety of exercises already discussed work the lats, including pullovers, parallel bar dips, and bent-over rowing. Two exercises particularly effective in developing the lats are pull-ups (pull-ups, chin-ups, and behind-the-neck pull-ups) and lat pulls.

Pull-ups Pull-ups can be done anywhere there is a bar on which to pull yourself up. There are pull-up bars in all gyms or playgrounds, or you can

Figure 5–9 *(a) Pull-ups, (b) chin-ups, and (c) behind-the-neck pull-ups*

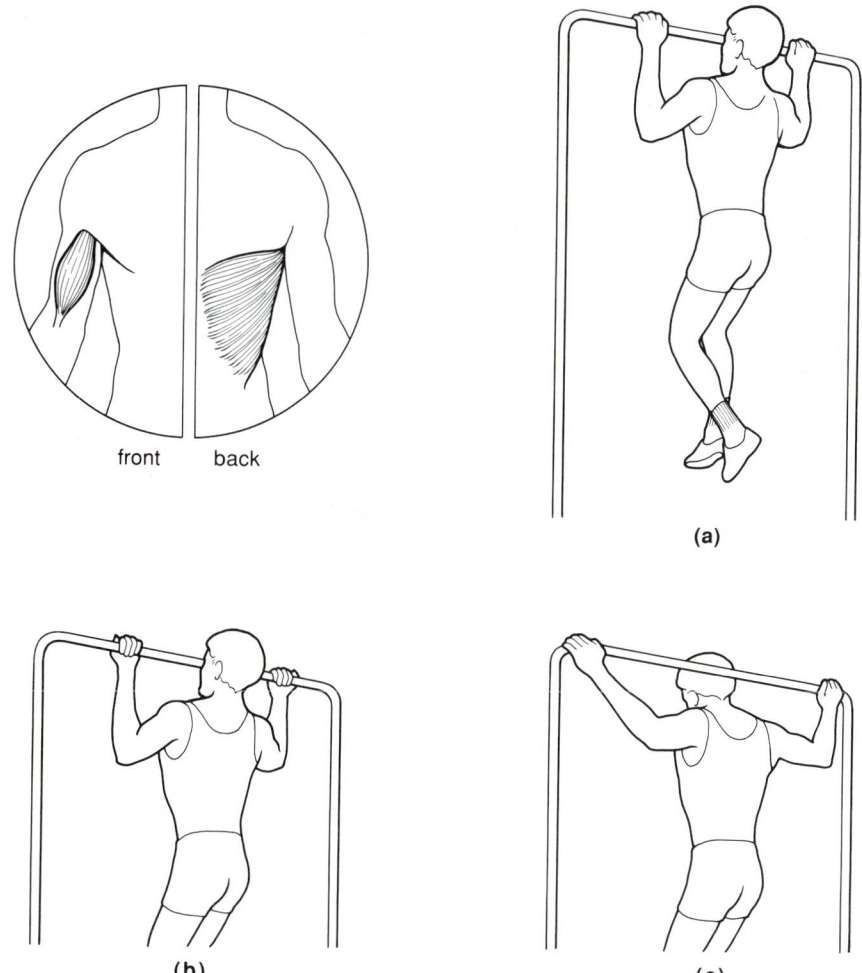

front   back

(a)

(b)   **(c)**

purchase one that can be mounted inside a doorway. Pull-ups, chin-ups, and behind-the-neck pull-ups are three variations of this exercise (Figure 5–9).

Pull-ups (pronated grip): Hang from a bar, elbows fully extended, using a pronated grip (palms away) and with your hands slightly more than shoulder width apart. Pull yourself up until your chin passes above the bar, then return to the starting position. Do not swing your legs during this exercise, and be sure to fully extend your elbows after each repetition. This exercise can be made more difficult by suspending weights from your weight lifting belt.

Chin-ups (supinated grip): This exercise is performed in exactly the same way as pull-ups except you use a supinated (hands toward you) grip. Chin-ups are easier to do than pull-ups, so they are a good exercise if you have difficulty performing the other forms of this exercise.

Behind-the-neck pull-ups: This exercise places more stress on the lats and is much more difficult to do than are the other kinds of pull-ups. Hang from a bar, using a pronated grip (palms away) with hands spread on the bar as far as possible from each other. Pull yourself up until the back of your neck makes contact with the bar, then return to the starting position.

Lat Pulls   Lat pulls require the use of a lat machine. This exercise is very similar to pull-ups, except that you pull weights down instead of pulling your body weight up (Figure 5–10). This exercise also develops the muscles on the front of your upper arm (biceps). To work the lats more, do the exercise using a wide grip; to work the biceps more, use a narrower grip.

Figure 5–10 *Lat pulls*

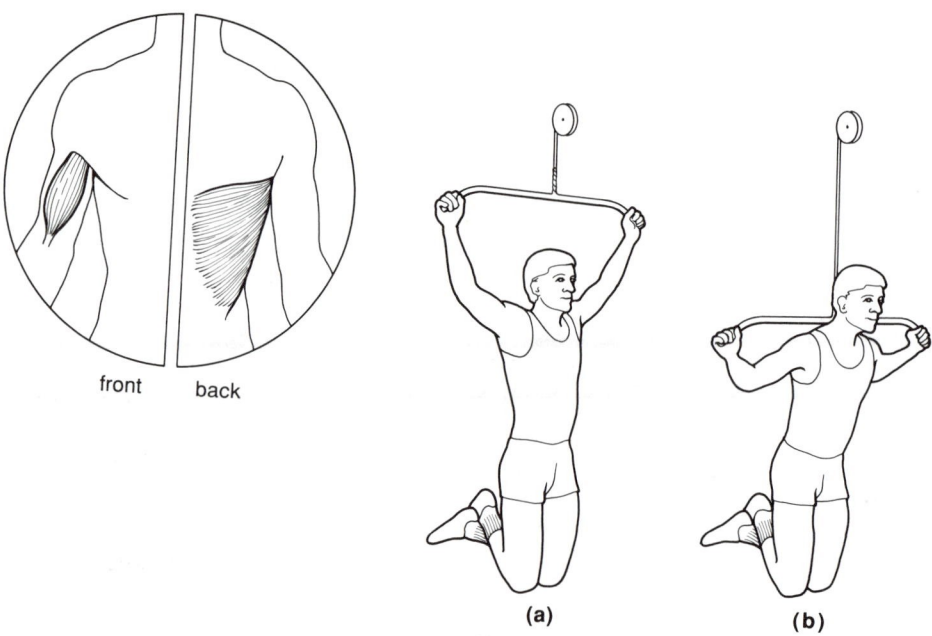

front   back

(a)   (b)

▶ The Technique: From a seated or kneeling position, grasp the bar of the lat machine using a pronated grip (palms away) with arms fully extended. Pull the weight down until it reaches near the back of your neck, then return to the starting position.

Take care not to touch your neck bones (vertebrae)   ◀ CAUTION
with the bar because you could injure them if you
mistakenly bang them too hard.

You can also do this exercise with a pronated grip (palms toward you), which places more stress on the biceps.

As you get stronger, a spotter may be required to hold you down during the exercise (Figure 5–11). The weight you use may exceed your body weight, and you will be pulled upward.

The spotter must take great care to keep his or her   ◀ CAUTION
head away from the bar to avoid being hit in the
event the lifter suddenly lets go of the bar.

Figure 5–11 *Spotting during lat pull exercise*

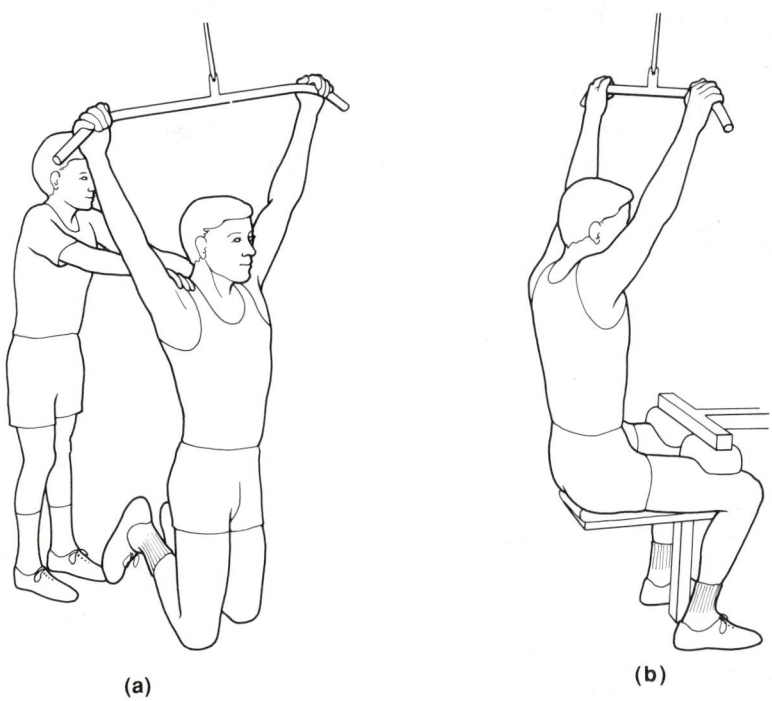

(a)   (b)

EXERCISES TO DEVELOP THE LOWER BACK

More than 85 percent of the U.S. population experiences back pain during their lifetime. Experts attribute some of this to poor strength and to inflexibility of the spinal muscles. A basic problem when selecting lower back exercises is that the best exercises for strengthening the lower back muscles are often the exercises that place the most stress on the spinal disks. Ideally, the lower back exercise program should build strong back muscles that help you achieve optimal spinal alignment and minimize pressure on the spinal nerves. The lower back muscles are well suited to helping you maintain an erect posture but poorly suited to lifting heavy objects.

Proper lifting techniques are essential for maintaining a healthy back. These techniques are detailed in Chapter 2. Other factors important to a healthy back include strong abdominal and leg muscles and flexible leg and back muscles. Regular aerobic exercise can also help prevent back pain.

Three types of lower back exercises are discussed in the next section:

1. Isometric extension exercises
2. Specific lower back weight training exercises
3. Weight training exercises that have a secondary effect on the lower back muscles

No lower back program is right for everyone. If a particular exercise causes you pain, stop doing it until you can seek professional advice. Circumstances change: an exercise that is inappropriate for you now may be good for you six months from now after a period of conditioning.

Isometric Extension Exercises

The purpose of isometric extension exercises is to strengthen the lower back muscles so that they are better able to maintain spinal alignment. Three exercises in this category include:

- ▶ Press-ups
- ▶ Unilateral spinal extensions
- ▶ Bilateral spinal extensions

Press-ups This exercise strengthens your lower back muscles and helps maintain the spine in a normal alignment. Press up on your hands while letting your lower back sag and attempt to keep your hips on the floor (Figure 5–12). Hold the position. Start with five seconds and gradually advance to thirty seconds per repetition.

Unilateral Spinal Extensions Balance on your right hand and knee (Figure 5–13). Lift your left leg and left arm. Extend your leg to the rear and

Figure 5–12 *The press-up*

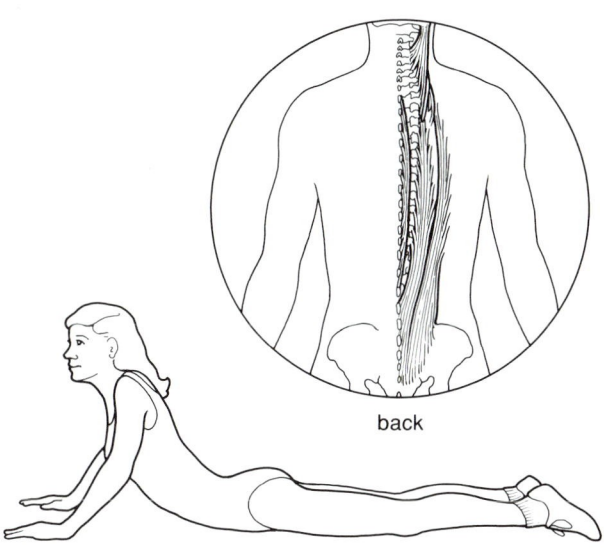

back

Figure 5–13 *(a) Unilateral back extensions, (b) bilateral back extensions*

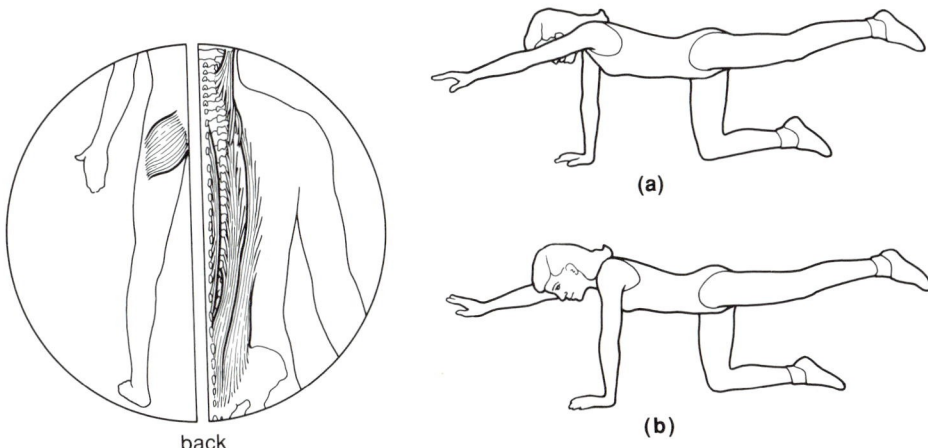

back

(a)

(b)

reach to the front with your arm. Hold this position for ten to thirty seconds. Repeat with your right leg and right arm. Start with five repetitions and advance to fifteen. This exercise can be made more difficult by attaching weights to your legs and arms. Ankle and wrist weights are inexpensive and can be purchased at any sporting goods store.

Bilateral Spinal Extensions Balance on your right hand and left knee (Figure 5–13). Lift your right leg and left arm. Extend your leg to the rear and reach to the front with your arm. Repeat with your left leg and right arm. Hold this position for ten to thirty seconds.

Exercises for the Lower Back

Including lower back weight training exercises in your program is a good idea if you also include squats and pulling exercises (cleans and snatches). Two popular lower back exercises are back extensions and good morning exercises.

Each of these exercises may subject the spinal disks to considerable pressure. If you are suffering from lower back pain, these exercises may do more harm than good. One popular lower back exercise, straight leg dead lifts, is not recommended because it creates excessive pressure on the spinal disks.

Back Extensions This exercise is often called back hyperextensions. It is not a good idea to extend too far backward during this exercise because you can put excessive pressure on the spinal disks.

▶ The Technique: Lie face down on a back extension bench with your upper body extending over the edge (Figure 5–14). Lower your upper body as far as you can, then lift your torso until it is again aligned with your legs.

Good Mornings This is a particularly good auxiliary exercise to a program that contains squats and pulling exercises.

▶ The Technique: Standing, place a barbell on your shoulders and flex your knees slightly (Figure 5–15). Bend at the waist while keeping your head up as much as possible, then return to the starting position. Do this exercise slowly and smoothly, and add weight very gradually. In general, do more reps (10–20) and use less weight than you normally would doing other weight training exercises.

Figure 5–14 *Back extensions*

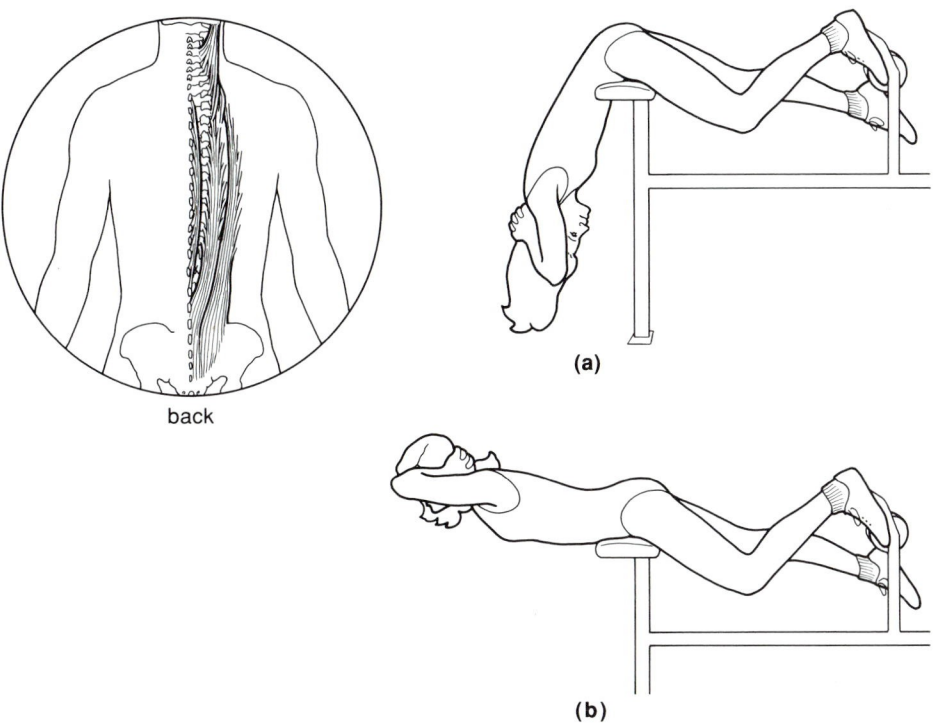

back

(a)

(b)

Figure 5–15 *The good morning exercise*

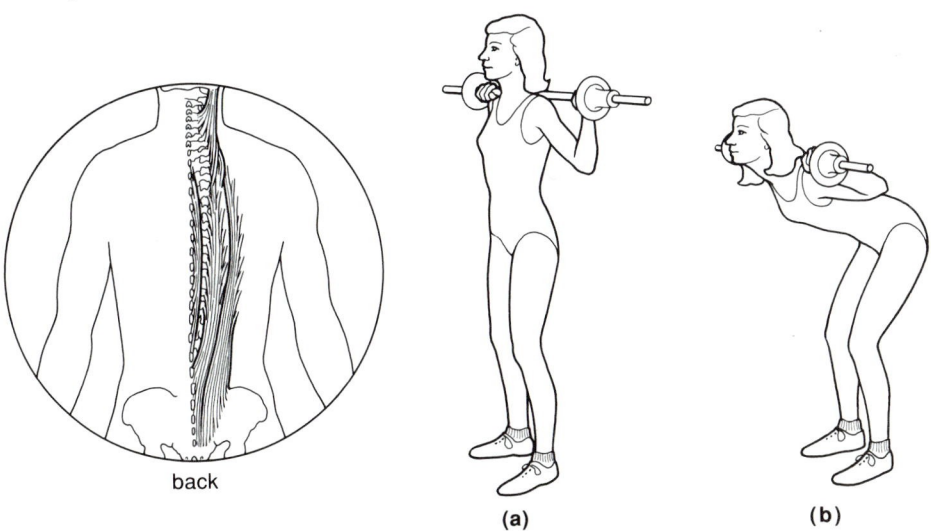

back

(a)   (b)

Exercises with a Secondary Effect on the Lower Back

Because the lower back is used to stabilize the upper body during many activities, almost all weight training exercises stress the lower back muscles to some extent. Exercises such as squats, cleans, and snatches are particularly good at developing lower back strength.

CAUTION ▶ Because these lifts actively involve the back, it is important to protect the back by wearing a weight lifting belt and by observing proper lifting techniques when performing the exercises.

▼

Exercises to Develop the Abdominal Muscles

Several years ago, a small book on developing a "flat" stomach made the best-seller list. People seem to be obsessed with having great-looking "abs." Well, there is some good news and some bad news about abdominal muscles. First, the bad news: many people, particularly men, naturally accumulate fat around the middle. No matter how much exercise you do, fat will remain there until you start to expend more calories than you are taking in. There is no such thing as spot reducing—you can't exercise muscles to lose the fat that lies over them.

Now, for the good news: the abdominal muscles are the major supporting structures of the abdomen. The legs and arms have large bones that provide structure; there are no such bones in the abdomen. Strong abdominal muscles add support to the midsection and act like a biological girdle to "hold you in." Stronger abdominal muscles make the area look tighter, even though the fat may still be there. The principle abdominal muscles include the rectus abdominis, which causes the trunk to bend or flex, and the obliques, which assist the rectus and allow you to rotate your trunk and bend to the side.

There is a wide variety of abdominal exercises. Many of these pose a danger to the neck and lower back and should be avoided. Dangerous abdominal exercises include straight leg sit-ups, double leg lifts, sit-ups with hands behind the head, and Roman chair sit-ups (Figure 6–1).

Straight leg sit-ups, Roman chair sit-ups, and double ◄ CAUTION
leg lifts place excessive stress on the intervertebral
disks, and sit-ups with hands behind the head could
injure the neck.

Figure 6–1 *Dangerous abdominal exercises*

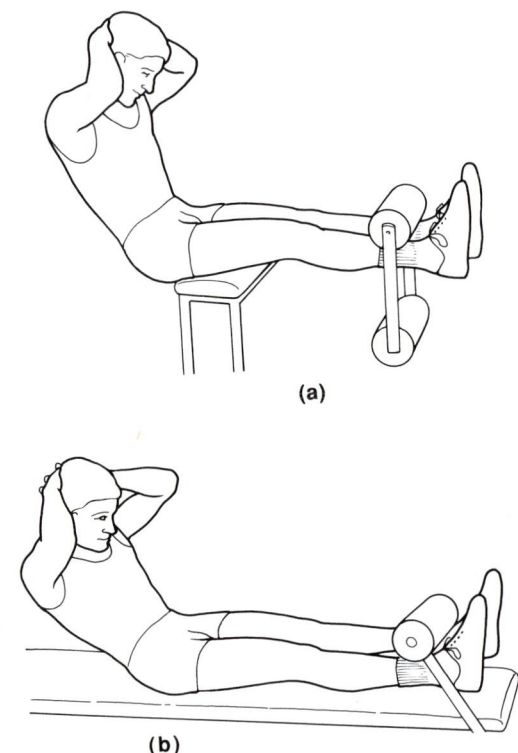

(a)

(b)

It is unlikely that doing a few sets of these exercises will cause immediate injury. Evidence suggests that chronically performing movements that place excessive stress on the disks eventually leads to disk deterioration and chronic back and neck pain. Avoid exercises that may cause problems. There are numerous exercises that are as effective as these dangerous ones for building the muscles of the trunk. These exercises include:

▶ Isometric abdominal exercise
▶ Crunches
▶ Sit-ups
▶ Hanging knee raises
▶ Twists

- ▶ Side-bends
- ▶ Reverse beetles

ABDOMINAL AND HIP FLEXOR WORKOUTS
Isometric Abdominal Exercise

Perhaps you're not aware that you have your own built-in abdominal exercise machine. The isometric abdominal exercise allows you to work on your abdominal muscles any time and anywhere. The exercise involves tightening your abdominal muscles isometrically for 10–30 seconds. Periodically during the day, hold your stomach in. You will notice a difference within a few weeks. Do not hold your breath while contracting your abdominal muscles isometrically, because this activity can restrict the blood flow to your heart and brain.

Crunches

Sports scientists have discovered that the abdominal muscles can get a tremendous workout by moving through a small range of motion. You don't need to do full-range-of-motion sit-ups to develop fully trained abdominals. Crunches are just as effective as sit-ups, and they place much less stress on your back.

Figure 6–2 *Crunches (abdominal curls)*

front

▶ The Technique: Lie on your back on the floor. Place your feet on the floor, on a bench, or extend your legs up a wall (Figure 6–2). With arms folded across your chest, curl your trunk toward your knees by raising your head and shoulders from the ground. Your back should remain stationary. The resistance can be increased by holding a weight plate on your chest.

Sit-Ups

Sit-ups are a basic exercise in almost everyone's program. Thirty years ago, sit-ups were done with straight legs. However, we've learned that straight leg sit-ups are not only hard on the back, but they also exercise a large hip flexor muscle group more than they exercise the abdominals. Recent studies suggest that holding your hands behind your head when doing sit-ups may cause neck injuries. Little of the exercise's value is lost by doing it with your arms folded across your chest or with your hands touching your ears.

Figure 6–3 *Sit-ups*

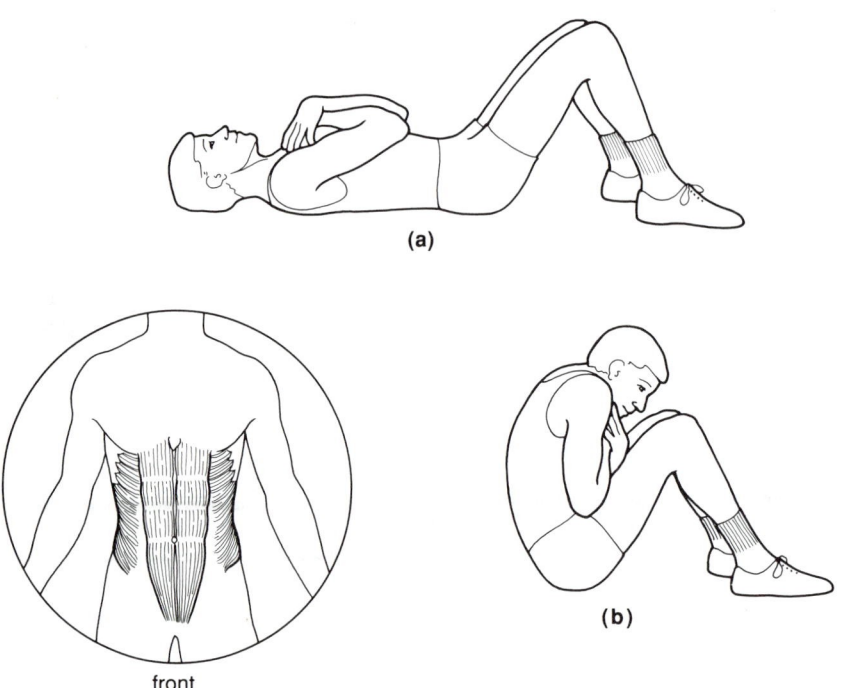

(a)

front

(b)

▶ The Technique: Lying on your back with knees bent, feet flat on the floor, and arms folded across your chest, bend at the waist and raise your head and shoulders toward your knees until your hands touch your thighs (Figure 6–3). Return to the starting position. You can modify this exercise to increase the stress on the obliques by twisting on the way up during the sit-up. As with crunches, the resistance can be increased by doing this exercise with weights.

Hanging Knee Raises

This exercise is performed hanging from a bar or from between two bars (such as found on the Universal Gym). It is a good exercise for the abdominal and hip flexor muscles.

▶ The Technique: While hanging from a bar, bring your knees up toward your chest, then return to the starting position (Figure 6–4).

Figure 6–4 *Hanging knee raises*

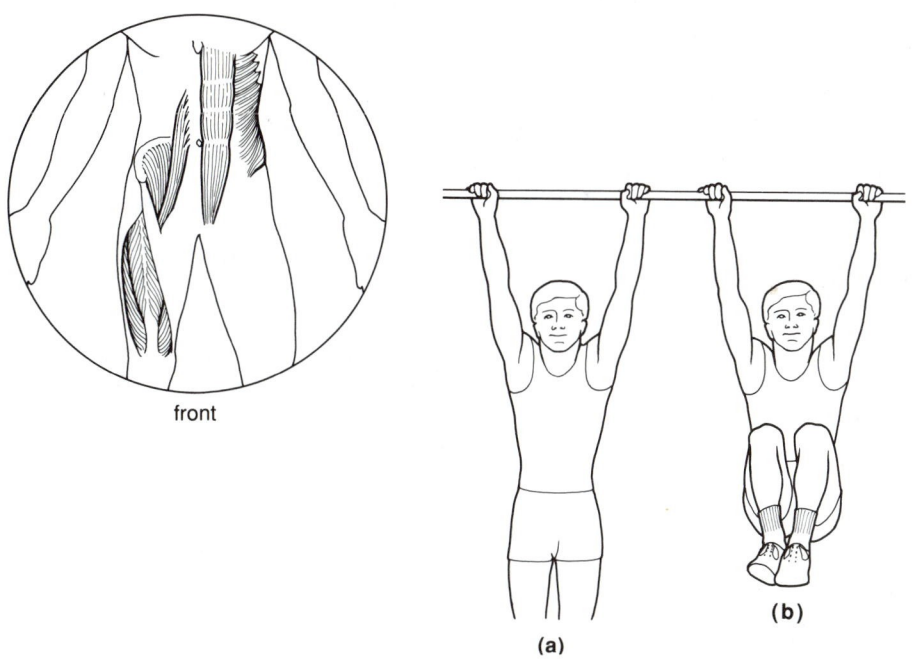

front

(a) (b)

WORKOUTS FOR THE OBLIQUES
Twists

Twists are a great way to exercise the obliques and make a dent in those "love handles." But remember, exercising specific body parts will only help to hold in the fat, not get rid of it. The obliques may look better, but the fat is still there.

▶ The Technique: From a seated or standing position, place a pole on your shoulders and rotate your trunk as far as possible, first to the left and then to the right (Figure 6–5). Later, you can use a barbell with weights to increase the resistance. Most people are more interested in definition than in size of the obliques. Do many repetitions of this exercise for definition. Several equipment manufacturers have developed machines that provide resistance during trunk rotation. Nevertheless, these machines are not yet widely available.

Side Bends

Side bends are another good exercise for developing the obliques. They can be done with dumbbells or floor pulleys.

▶ The Technique: From a standing position and holding a barbell in one hand, lean over to that side as far as possible, then return to the starting position (Figure 6–6). Repeat this exercise on the other side of the body.

Reverse Beetles

This exercise received its name because when weight-trainers do it, they resemble beetles that have been turned over on their backs. Reverse beetles can be modified to increase the stress on the obliques by twisting as you do them.

▶ The Technique: From a seated position on a bench, curl your trunk by bringing your knees and shoulders together (Figure 6–7). Then straighten your legs and move your shoulders backward. Several equipment manufacturers make an exercise machine that simulates this exercise.

Figure 6–5 *Twists*

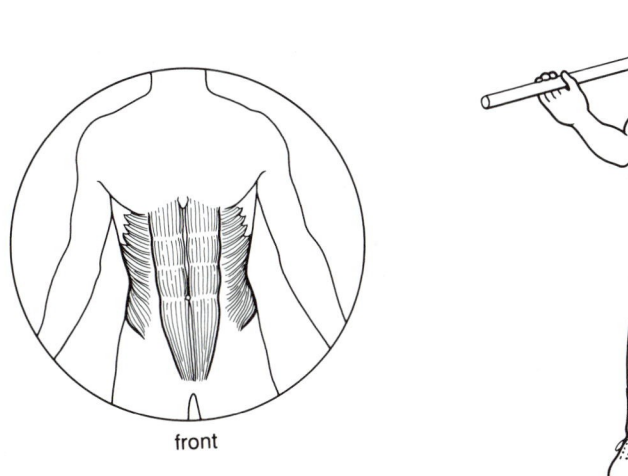

front

Figure 6–6 *Side bends*

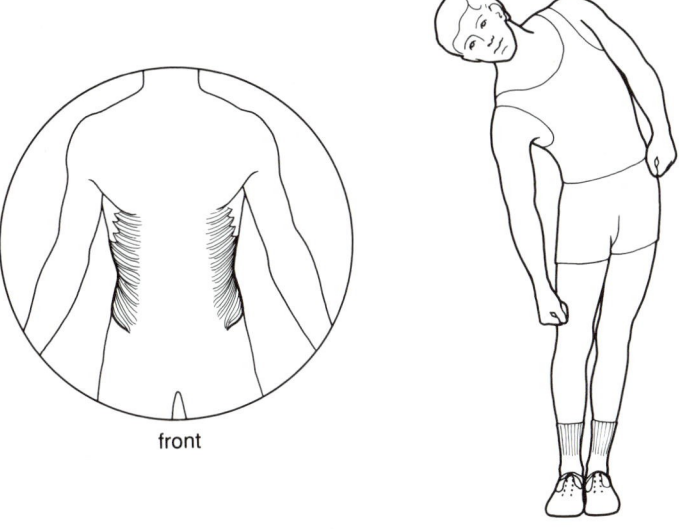

front

Figure 6–7 *Reverse beetles*

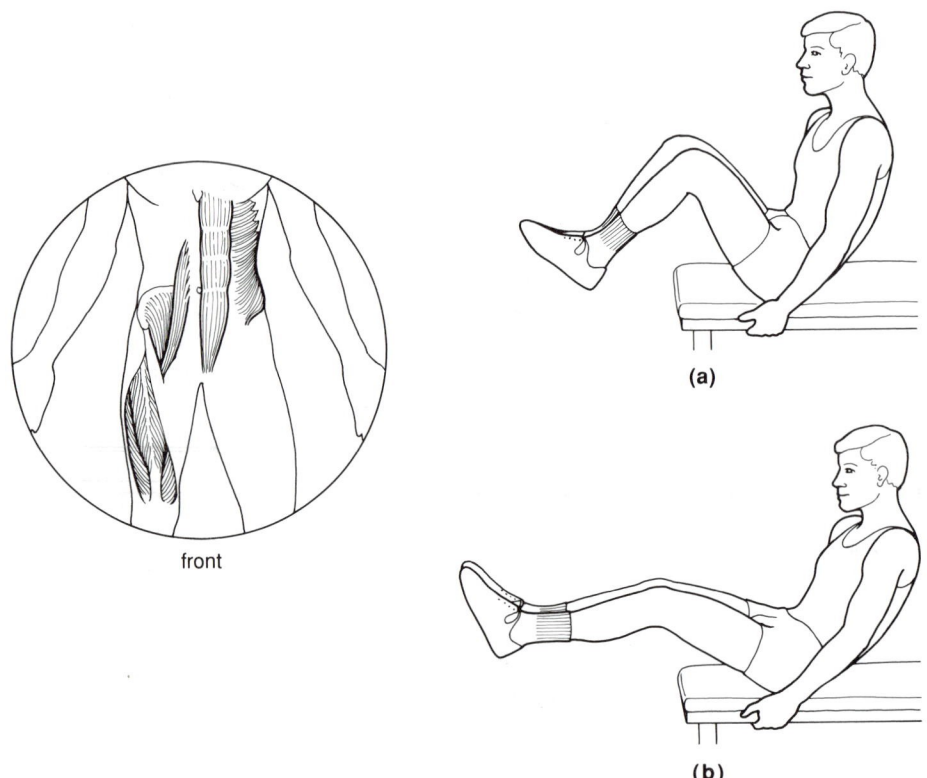

front

(a)

(b)

ABDOMINAL EXERCISE MACHINES

Many kinds of abdominal exercise machines have been developed over the last five years. Most equipment manufacturers have taken pains to ensure that these machines protect the back and are adjustable to different body sizes. They are available in better equipped gyms and health clubs.

▼

CHAPTER SEVEN

Exercises for the Lower Body

If you were interested in developing strength and power in sports, and had to choose one part of the body to exercise over all others, you should choose the lower body. Many athletes spend long hours working on their bench press and arm size, while doing few lower body exercises. An old saying among weight trainers is "if you can't squat, then you ain't strong." It makes no sense to have powerful chest and arm muscles and a bird-like lower body. Your legs won't be able to support the rest of your body's strength.

The leg muscles are the largest and most powerful in the body. Most athletic movements require that power be initiated with the muscles of the legs and hips. For example, golfers, batters, javelin throwers, and tennis players initiate movement with their legs and finish the movement with their upper bodies. Those failing to use the lower body effectively, relying instead on the weaker and more fragile upper body muscles, perform ineffectively and are more prone to injury. Figure 7–1 shows the basic athletic position used in sports such as tennis, football, racketball, and wrestling. The legs are bent and the center of gravity is low. The person can easily move in any direction and has good stability. Movement is much easier and more effective if the lower body muscles are strong and powerful.

This chapter discusses three exercise categories for developing strength, power, and muscle growth in the lower body, including squats and leg presses, multi-joint exercises (where force is initially generated from the legs), and auxiliary leg strengthening exercises. As discussed in Chapter 1, every program designed to develop strength and power for sports should contain presses, pulls, and squats. Pulls and squats are mainly lower body exercises.

Figure 7–1 *Basic athletic position*

MULTI-JOINT LOWER BODY EXERCISES

Squats and leg presses are multi-joint exercises involving the knee and hip joints. They develop strength that can improve performance in most sports. They also increase strength, to a certain extent, in the back and abdominal muscles. Lifts included in this category are:

- ▶ Squats and leg presses
- ▶ Bench squats
- ▶ Power rack squats
- ▶ Front squats
- ▶ Hack squats
- ▶ Rack squats
- ▶ Lunges

Squats and Leg Presses

Many people avoid squats because of reports that deep knee bends overstretch the knee ligaments. In fact, you can squat very low before the knee ligaments are stretched significantly. Good form is essential in this lift. Beginners very often use too much weight; consequently, they bend their backs excessively during the lift and may injure themselves.

▶ The Technique: Most experts recommend using a weight lifting belt when doing squats. Begin the exercise (Figure 7–2) standing with your feet shoulder width apart and toes pointed slightly outward, the bar resting on the back of your shoulders, and with your hands holding the bar in that position. Keep your head up and lower back straight. Squat down (under control) until your thighs are approximately parallel with the floor and gluteals are about one inch below the knee. Drive upward toward the starting position, keeping your back in a fixed position throughout the exercise. A general strategy for this lift is to go down slow and up fast.

Figure 7–2 *The squat*

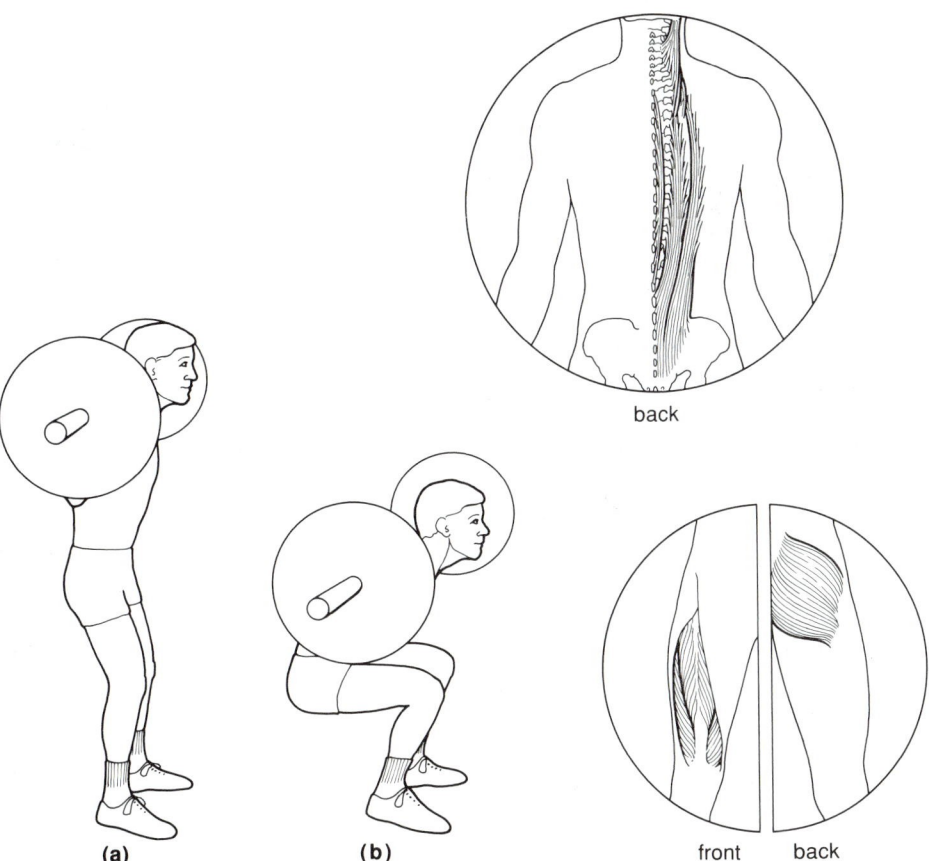

back

(a)   (b)

front   back

CAUTION ► Never "bounce" at the bottom of the squat because this might cause injury to the ligaments of your knee.

Safety should be of primary concern. A good squat rack is an important prerequisite. The rack should be sturdy and adjustable to individuals of different heights. Some racks have a safety bar at the bottom that can be used if the lift cannot be completed. Spotters are also required. Two spotters, standing on either side of the lifter, should be prepared to assist in the event that the lifter fails to complete a repetition. Weight belts are recommended. Some lifters wrap their knees and use weight-lifting boots to provide added support.

Figure 7–3 *The bench squat*

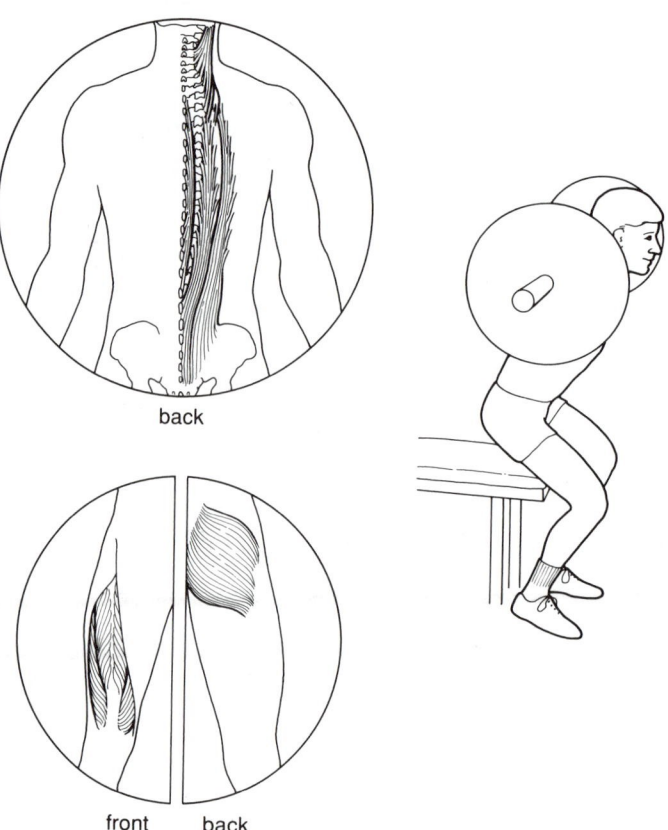

back

front   back

There are many variations to this exercise that can be substituted or supplemented to increase squatting power. These include bench squats and power rack squats.

Bench Squats Bench squats involve squatting down until you contact the bench, then returning to the starting position (Figure 7–3). Using a bench that prevents you from going to the parallel position will allow you to use more weight.

A danger of using a bench is that you may slam down ◄ CAUTION
on it during the exercise and injure your intervertebral
disks. For this reason it is important not to bounce
off the bench when doing bench squats.

Some weight training experts do not recommend bench squats because of danger to the spine if the exercises are not done properly.

Power Rack Squats Power rack squats allow you to use the power rack to overcome sticking points in the range of motion. As with the power rack bench press exercise described in Chapter 3, select three positions along the range of motion used during the squat (Figure 7–4). The first peg should be placed so that your thighs are nearly parallel with the ground. With the bar resting on your shoulders and on the first pegs, push the weight upward until you are standing upright. After you have completed your workout at the first peg, move the peg so that the bar lies in the middle of the range of motion. Repeat the exercise sequence. Finally, move the pegs so that the bar travels only a few inches during the exercise. At this peg stop, you will be capable of handling much more weight than you can from the parallel squat position.

Leg Presses Leg presses are done on leg press exercise machines and can be substituted for squats. They are safer and more convenient to do than squats because they don't involve handling weights, they place less stress on the back, and they don't require a spotter. Leg presses, however, are less effective than squats for developing strength in the quadriceps, gluteals, and hamstrings.

Figure 7–4 *Power rack squat*

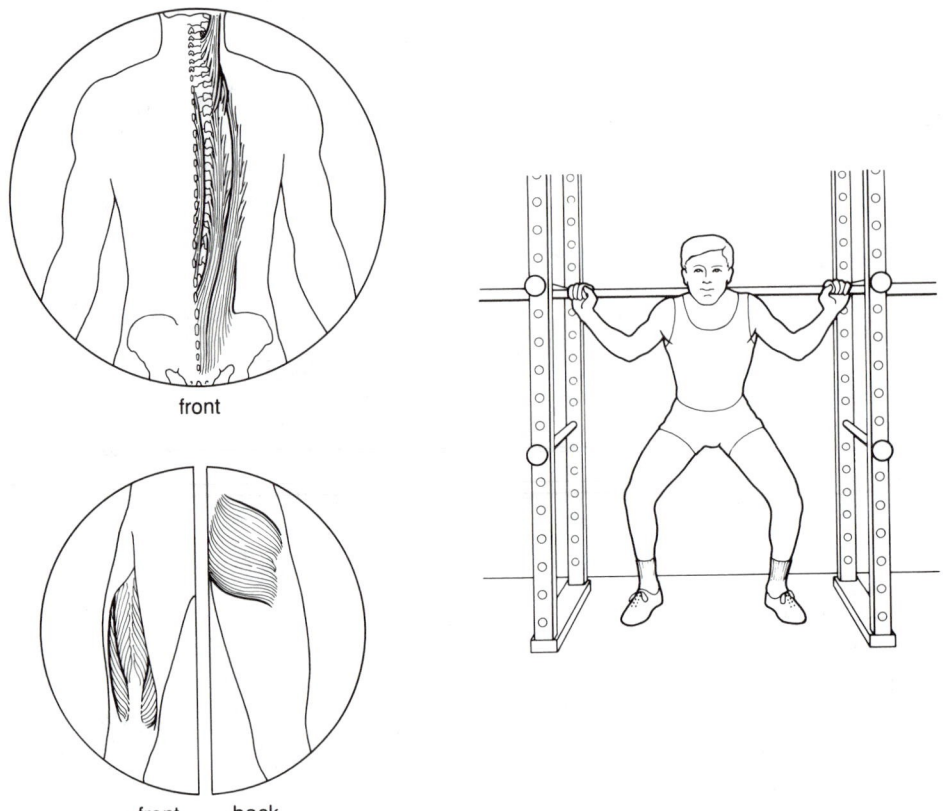

front

front   back

Front Squats

Front squats are a variation of the squat that is used mainly in training programs of Olympic style weight-lifters. During the lift, the bar is rested on the chest (such as when doing an overhead press). This lift better isolates the legs because the back cannot be used as much to assist in the movement. Consequently, you cannot lift as much weight in this exercise as in regular squats.

▶ The Technique: Standing with your feet shoulder width apart and toes pointed slightly outward, hold the bar on your chest, and squat down

Figure 7–5 *Front squats*

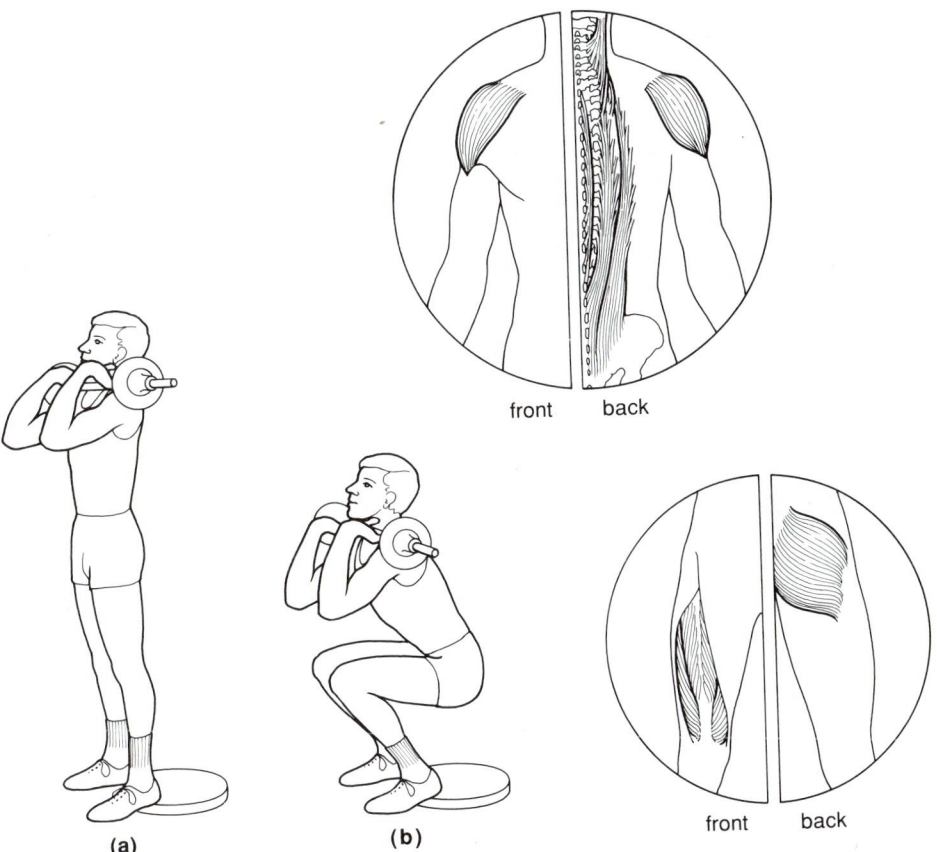

until your gluteals are one inch below the knee (Figure 7–5). Do this exercise in a controlled manner because you can easily lose your balance. Stability can sometimes be improved by placing small weight plates (5-lb plate) under your heels.

Hack Squats

Hack squats also isolate the thigh muscles more than squats because they force you to keep your back straighter—even more so than during front squats. This exercise is generally used as an auxiliary to squats rather than as the primary leg exercise.

▶ The Technique: From a standing position, hold a barbell behind you with your arms fully extended down so the weight rests on the back of your thighs (Figure 7–6). Slowly squat until the weight nearly reaches the ground, then push up to the starting position.

Figure 7–6 *Hack squats*

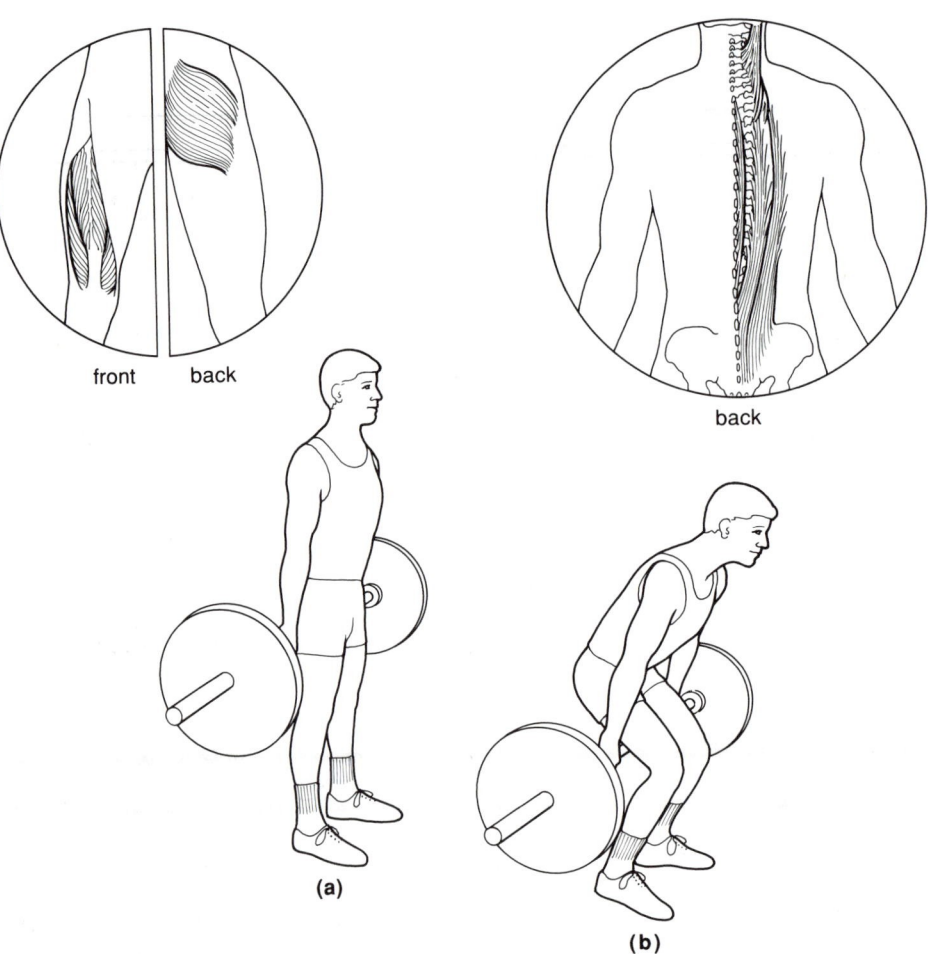

Rack Squats

Some equipment manufacturers make squat rack machines that enable you to push the weight up at about a 65 degree angle. These are excellent for simulating the movement used by football linemen and are valuable supplements or replacements for squats in the exercise program.

Lunges

Lunges are a great exercise for the quadriceps (front thigh), gluteus maximus (buttocks), and, to a lesser extent, the calf (back of lower leg) and lower back muscles.

▶ The Technique: Begin standing with your feet shoulder width apart and the bar resting on the back of your shoulders, with your hands holding the bar in that position (Figure 7–7). Lunge forward with one leg, bending it

Figure 7–7 *Lunges*

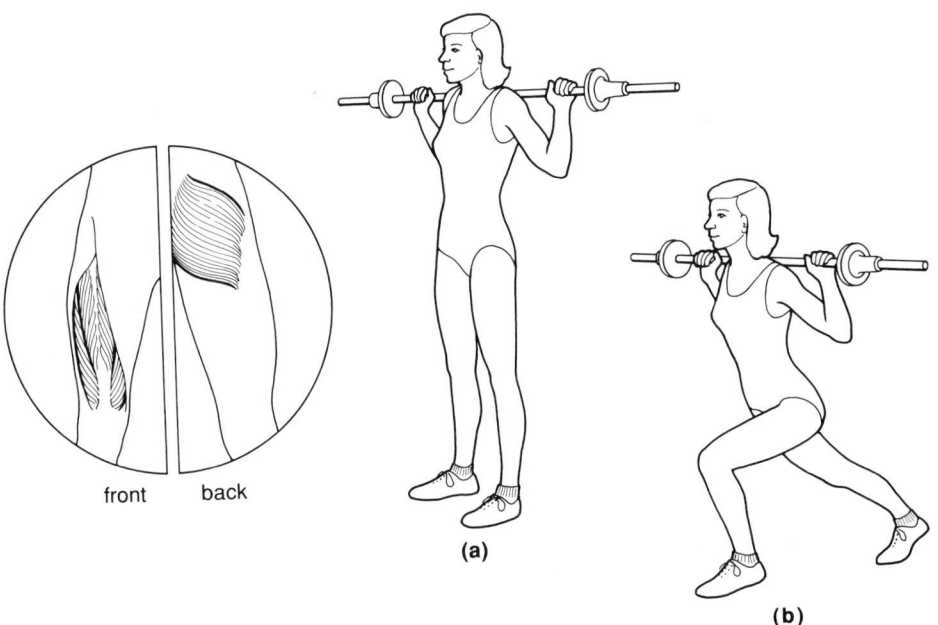

front   back

(a)

(b)

until the thigh is parallel to the floor. Repeat the exercise using the other leg. Keep your back and head as straight as possible, and maintain control while performing the exercise.

Isokinetic Squat Machines

Another relatively new product is the high speed squat machine. These machines are constructed so that resistance is added to the movement when you are traveling relatively fast. They present a tremendous risk of injury and have no place in the weight room.

CAUTION ►   Sudden loading of the spine at high speeds may cause severe damage to the intervertebral disks. High speed squat machines are not recommended.

MULTI-JOINT EXERCISES WHERE FORCE IS INITIALLY GENERATED BY THE LEGS

These exercises are popular with serious weight trainers. They are complex exercises that take a considerable amount of time to learn. They are very valuable because they develop strength from the basic athletic position and help improve strength and power for many sports. These exercises include:

► Power cleans
► High pulls
► Dead lifts
► Push presses

Power Cleans and High Pulls

Power cleans are used to get the weight to the starting position for the overhead press exercise (see Chapter 3). It should be a central exercise in the program of strength–speed athletes such as football players, throwers (shot-put, discus, hammer, and javelin), volleyball players, and wrestlers.

Figure 7–8 *Power cleans*

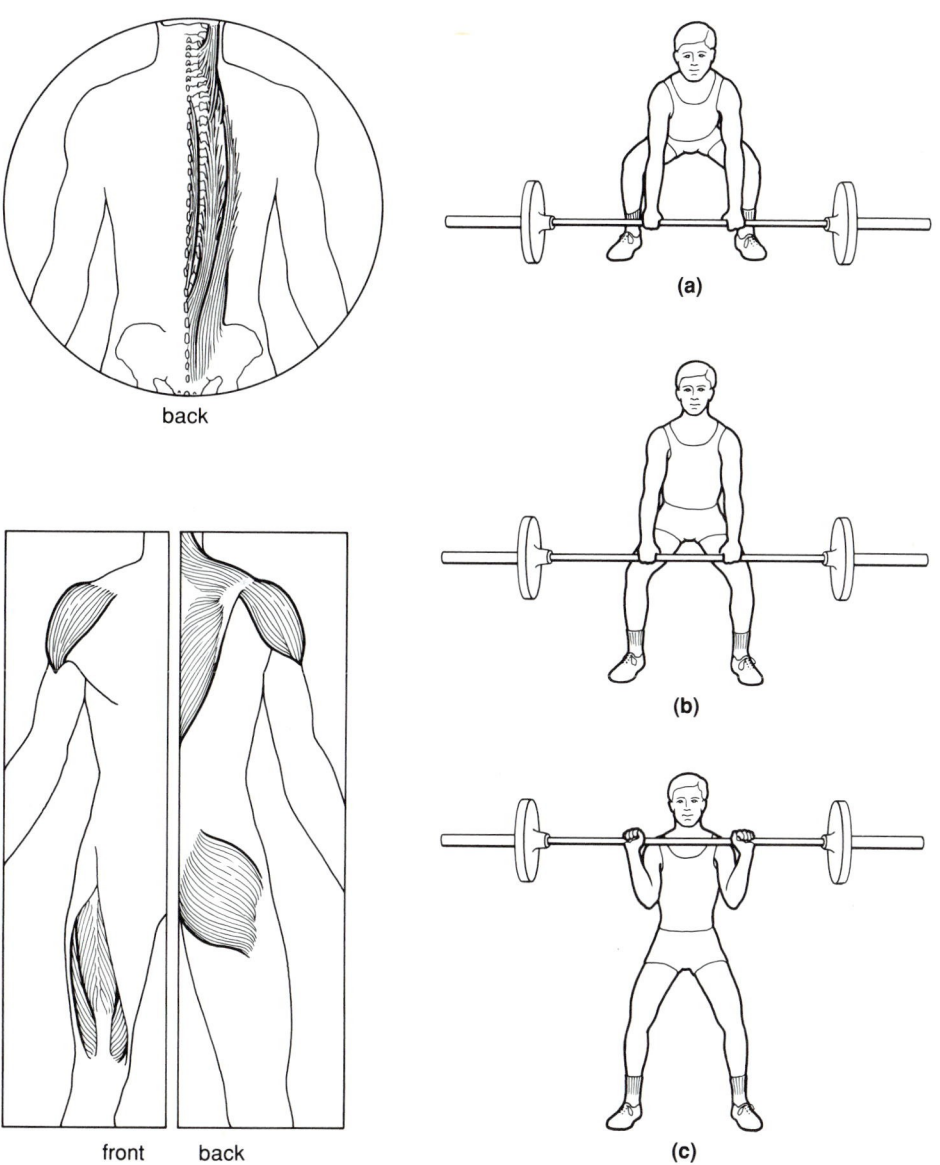

back

front   back

(a)

(b)

(c)

▶ The Technique: Place the bar on the floor in front of your shins. Keep your feet approximately two feet apart. Grasp the bar with your hands at shoulder width with your palms down (pronated grip) and squat, keeping your arms and back straight and your head up (Figure 7–8). Pull the weight up past your knees to your chest while throwing your hips forward and shoulders back. The main power for this exercise should come from your hips and legs. Return the bar to the starting position.

Figure 7–9 *High pull*

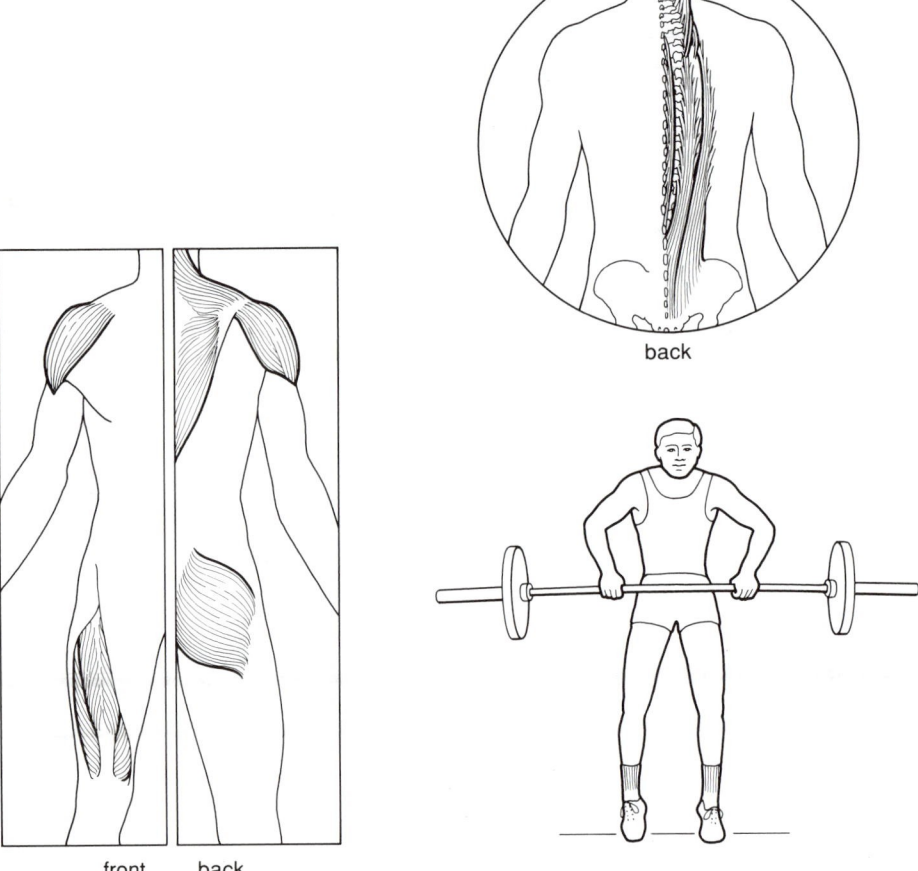

back

front   back

Variations of this lift include the high pull (Figure 7–9), squat clean, and split clean. The high pull is identical to the power clean, except that you don't turn the bar over at the top of the lift and catch it at your chest. This procedure allows you to handle more weight and place less stress on your wrists and forearms. The squat clean and split clean, which are beyond the scope of this book, are used in Olympic weight lifting (a form of competitive weight lifting) and take a long time to learn. The snatch (an Olympic lift) is another pulling exercise that is extremely difficult for the novice to master.

Dead Lifts

The dead lift is one of the three power lifts (a weight lifting competition event; the other two power lifts are the bench press and squat). It is an excellent exercise for the legs and back. Because it is possible to handle so much weight in this exercise, it is critical that proper form be maintained to avoid injury to the back.

▶ The Technique: Place the bar on the floor in front of your shins. Keep your feet approximately shoulder width apart. Grasp the bar with your hands at shoulder width, using a dead lift grip (one hand pronated and one hand supinated, see Chapter 2) and squat down, keeping your arms and back straight and your head up (Figure 7–10). Pull the weight past your knees until you are in a fully erect position. Return the weight to the floor under control, being careful to bend only your knees and maintain a straight back.

AUXILIARY EXERCISES FOR THE LOWER BODY

A number of auxiliary exercises for the lower body isolate specific muscle groups such as the quadriceps (front of thigh), hamstrings (back of thigh), and calfs (back of lower leg). Auxiliary exercises include:

▶ Knee extensions
▶ Knee flexions (leg curls)
▶ Heel raises

Figure 7–10 *Dead lift*

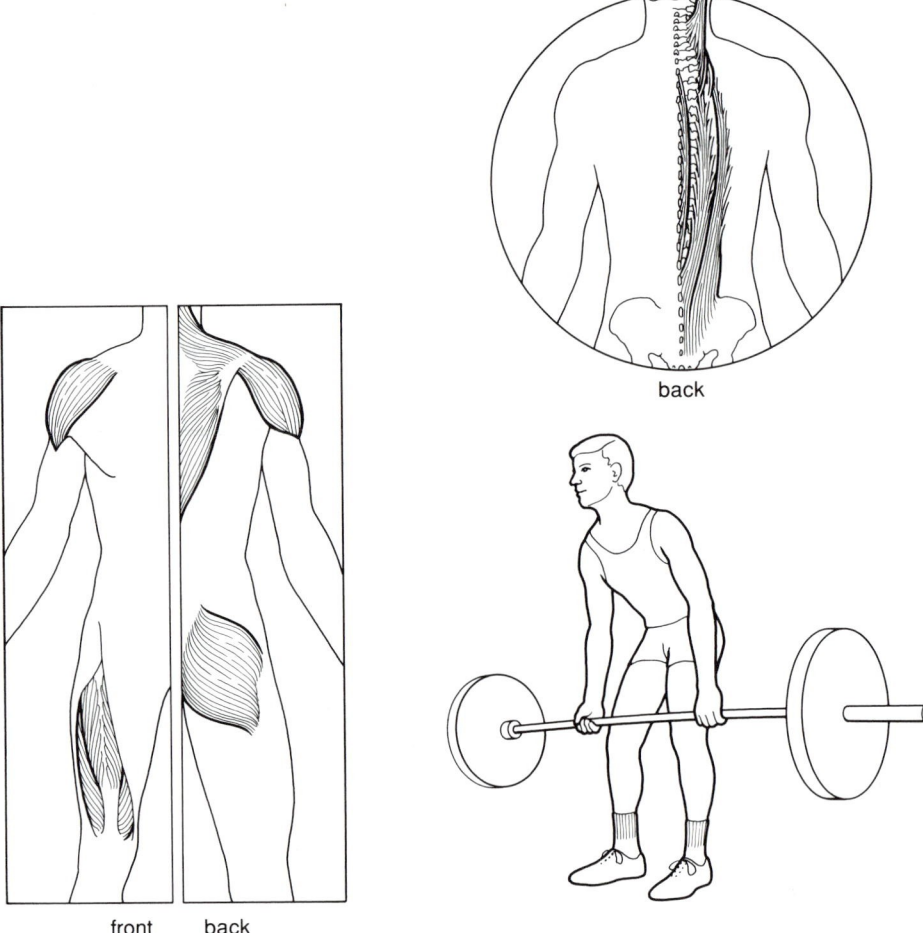

back

front   back

Knee Extensions

Knee extensions are done on a knee extension machine found in most gyms. Knee extensions using weighted boots are not recommended because they may place excessive stress on the ligaments of the knee. Knee extensions are excellent for building the quadriceps muscle group. They are good for supplementing squats or leg presses in the general program. If

Figure 7–11 *Knee extensions*

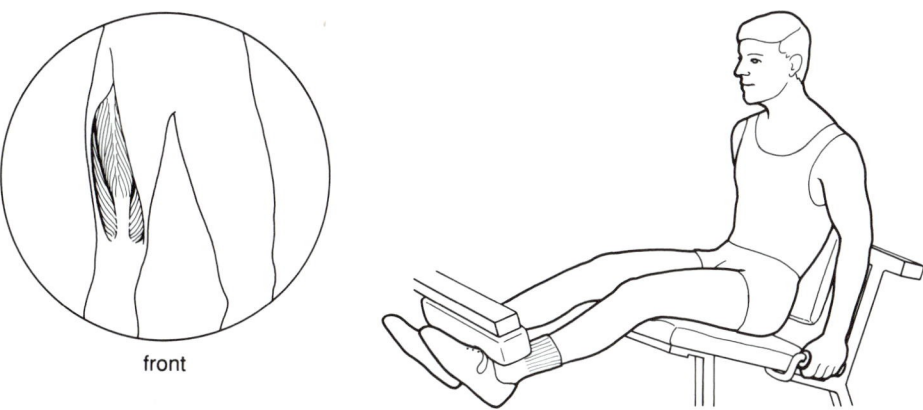

front

you experience pain under or around your knee cap during the exercise or within a day or two of doing this exercise, stop doing knee extensions until you can check with your coach. This exercise must be modified or eliminated from the programs of people with knee cap pain.

▶ The Technique: Sit on the knee extension bench and place the front of your shins on the knee extension pads (Figure 7–11). Extend your knees until they are straight, then return to the starting position.

Knee Flexions (Leg Curls)

Knee flexions are more commonly known as leg curls and require the use of a leg curl machine. This exercise develops the hamstrings, the muscles on the back of your thighs.

▶ The Technique: Lie on your stomach, resting the pads of the machine just below your calf muscles (Figure 7–12). Flex your knees until they approach your buttocks, then return to the starting position. Because the hamstrings are weaker than the quadriceps, you will be unable to handle as much weight on this exercise as on the knee extension machine. Most sports build the quadriceps muscles, but few work on the hamstrings. Injuries can be caused by imbalances between muscles on the front and

Figure 7–12 *Knee flexions (leg curls)*

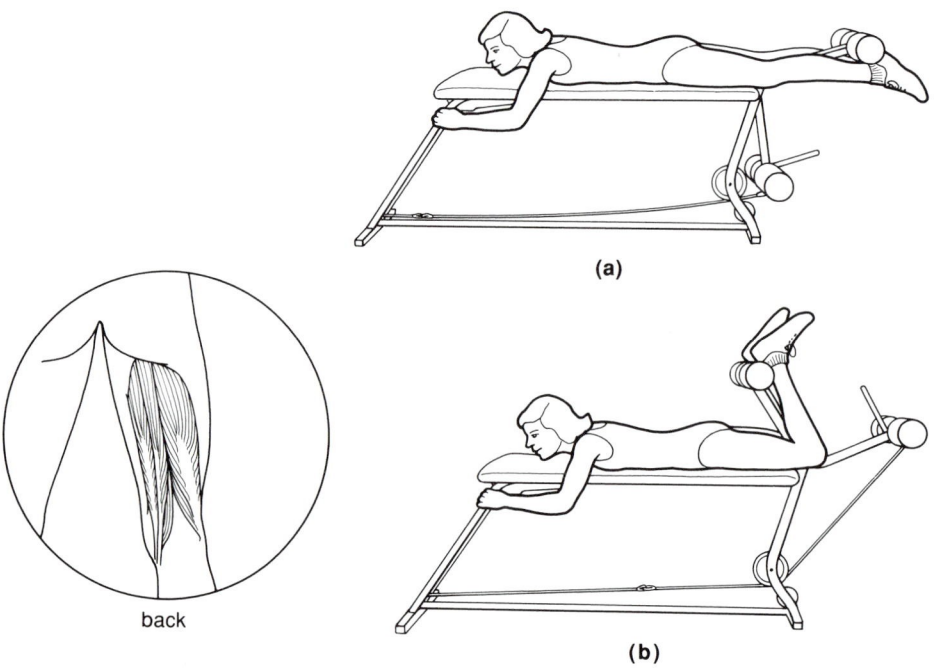

(a)

(b)

back

backs of your legs. It is important to work on your hamstrings in addition to your quadriceps to maintain a balance.

Heel Raises

Heel raises strengthen the calf muscles (muscles on the back of the lower leg—soleus, gastrocnemius, and plantaris) and the Achilles tendon (the tendon connecting the calf muscles to the heel). These exercises can be done anywhere there is a step or block of wood and do not necessarily require weights.

▶ The Technique: Standing on the edge of a stair or block of wood with a barbell resting on your shoulders, slowly lower your heels as far as possible, then raise them until you are up on your toes (Figure 7–13). The calf

Figure 7–13 *Heel raises*

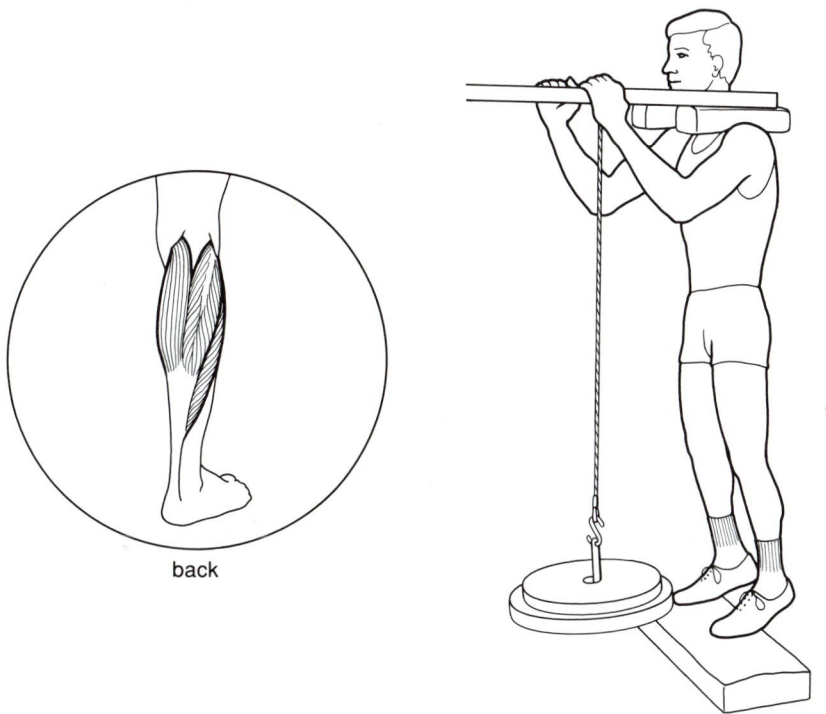

back

muscles are very strong and require a great deal of resistance to increase their size and strength. Calf exercises can be added at the end of your squat or leg press routine. Do heel raises after you have completed the last repetition of leg exercise.

Calf Machines Most gyms have some kind of exercise machine for the calfs. Usually these are more effective than doing heel raises because they are safer and easier to do. On the machines, you usually don't have to handle weights or worry about balance while carrying a lot of weight.

▼

CHAPTER EIGHT

Nutrition for Weight Trainers

Nutrition plays an important role in maximizing the effects of a weight training and physical fitness program. Scientists are beginning to appreciate the role of diet and nutritional manipulation in athletic success. Although the balanced diet is still the cornerstone of the well-rounded fitness program, various dietary techniques are effective in improving performance.

Be cautious of nutritional advice that seems too good to be true. No nutritional supplement or drug will turn a weak, flabby person into a sleek, muscular athlete. Those changes require hard work and dedication. Instant "cures" such as mega–vitamin therapy or anabolic steroids usually don't work and are either dangerous or expensive. You are better off staying with the proven principles of nutrition and participating in a steady, progressive fitness program.

THE BALANCED DIET: CORNERSTONE OF THE SUCCESSFUL FITNESS PROGRAM

Billions of dollars are spent each year in the United States on diet foods and food supplements. These products include artificial sweeteners, vitamin pills, protein supplements, amino acid pills, and diet sodas. Yet, it is difficult to improve upon sensible eating habits for maximizing the effects of your fitness program and maintaining a trim, attractive body. A balanced diet plays a critical role in any fitness–nutrition program. This diet provides all of the known nutrients, reduces the risk of coronary artery disease, and provides enough energy to sustain a vigorous lifestyle. The balanced diet consists of at least three meals a day of foods from the seven basic groups:

- ▶ Milk and milk products (including yogurt, cottage cheese, and ice cream)
- ▶ Protein foods (including lean meat, fish, poultry, cheese, eggs, and beans)
- ▶ Vitamin C fruits and vegetables (including citrus and tomatoes)
- ▶ Dark green and yellow vegetables
- ▶ Potatoes and other starchy vegetables
- ▶ Whole grain products (including bread and cereals)
- ▶ Fats (margarine and vegetable oils)

The seven basic food groups are an extension of the four basic food groups first suggested by the United States Department of Agriculture in 1957. The "basic four" was extended to the "basic seven" for the purpose of getting people to eat fewer meat and dairy products containing cholesterol and saturated fats and more fruits, vegetables, and cereals.

The well-balanced diet satisfies the nutritional requirements stipulated in the Recommended Daily Allowances (RDA) of the National Research Council of the National Academy of Sciences. The RDA are based upon current research on nutrition but, obviously, do not account for nutrients whose requirements have not yet been established. Therefore, you should always eat a variety of foods from the basic food groups. Remember, all the food supplements in the world are not going to make up for a poor diet. You cannot get optimal nutrition from a pill.

Milk and milk products are important sources of calcium, riboflavin, high-quality protein, carbohydrate, fat, and other vitamins and minerals. Protein foods (such as meats, chicken, and fish), in addition to supplying protein, also supply iron, thiamin, riboflavin, niacin, phosphorus, and zinc. Avoid eating meats with a high fat content because they are associated with increased risk of heart disease.

The cereals, starch, and fat groups supply energy, thiamin, iron, niacin, and cellulose (fiber). These groups are critical for satisfying the energy requirements of a vigorous exercise program. The fruit and vegetable groups are important for supplying vitamins, minerals, and fiber. It is particularly important to eat dark green and deep yellow vegetables because of their high nutrient content and their possible influence in reducing the risk of certain types of cancer.

Fluids are a particularly important part of an active person's diet because they directly affect exercise capacity. Body water is an important component in most of the body's biochemical reactions and helps maintain blood volume and control body temperature. A variety of effective fluid replacements, designed for active people, have been developed that not only satisfy the body's fluid requirements but also provide energy during exercise and hasten recovery following a vigorous workout.

VITAMINS

Large amounts of money are spent on vitamin–mineral pills every year by athletes and nonathletes. Yet, the only common documented deficiency in the United States is iron deficiency. The bulk of the research on vitamin supplementation suggests, with a few possible exceptions, that anything more than a balanced diet and, perhaps, a one-a-day type pill is useless and a waste of your money.

Vitamins act as co-enzymes (they work with enzymes to drive the body's metabolism) and aid in the production and protection of red blood cells. While vitamins are required by the body in extremely small amounts, they are not produced in the body and must be consumed in the diet. Of all the body's vitamins, only vitamin C, thiamin, pyridoxine, and riboflavin are affected by exercise. Of these, only vitamin C supplementation has been shown to improve performance, and that was in vitamin C deficient adolescents.

Vitamin C supplementation has been a fertile area of debate since Linus Pauling suggested megadoses of the vitamin as a cure for the common cold. His contention has been extremely controversial, and in general, medical research has not supported his claims. Recent, well-controlled studies conducted at the University of Wisconsin Medical School have shown that vitamin C may indeed prevent the spread of colds and decrease the severity of symptoms. This could be good news for active people because preventing the down-time from illness is just as effective as discovering a new ergogenic aid (substances that enhance performance). Certainly there will be continued debate on this issue for many years.

Overall, it appears that vitamin supplements improve performance only if there is a nutritional deficiency. To be on the safe side, you might consider taking a basic vitamin supplement. You might also take some additional vitamin C in case it really does prevent the common cold. As long as you don't overdo it, the extra vitamin C probably won't hurt you and may help you. There does not appear to be any justification for the mega-doses of vitamins taken by many athletes and other physically active people.

Many active people, particularly women, can benefit from iron supplementation. As many as 80 percent of women endurance athletes may be iron deficient. Athletes lose a lot of iron through feces, urine, sweat, and menstrual blood. Iron intake in athletes is often inadequate. This leads to a drop in iron stores in the bone marrow and, eventually, to iron deficient anemia. Iron deficiency results in impaired performance and fatigue. Iron supplements are beneficial to the person who is iron deficient and can have a marked effect on the endurance capacity and the ability to transport oxygen.

ENERGY REQUIREMENTS OF ACTIVE PEOPLE

The vast majority of body functions, including muscle contractions that allow us to lift weights and perform all other physical tasks, are driven by the energy supplied by the foods we eat. Carbohydrates, fats, and proteins constitute the three basic food components. Of these, carbohydrates and fats are vital for supplying the body's energy needs during exercise.

Active people must take in enough calories to satisfy the energy requirements of physical activity and must provide for themselves the nutrients necessary for optimal health. Again, this can be accomplished by following a well-balanced diet that contains enough calories to satisfy the body's needs but not so many that you become overweight.

Muscle Glycogen and Performance

Carbohydrates are the most important fuel for muscular work. Carbohydrates supply increased energy requirements with increased intensity of physical activity. When your muscles are depleted of glycogen (the body's energy storage molecule), fatigue and sluggishness set in. Glycogen use increases with the intensity of the exercise. Depletion of muscle glycogen limits performance and causes fatigue in people participating in endurance exercise, such as running, and in strength exercise, such as weight training.

Glycogen, the principal carbohydrate used during exercise, is stored mainly in the muscles and liver. The amount of glycogen present when exercise begins determines endurance time, the capacity for intense exercise, and mental attitude toward an intense workout or competition. If your muscles feel tired, you are not likely to have a very effective workout. Glycogen depletion is associated with fatigue, and if normal glycogen levels are not restored, physical performance levels will be impaired. The goal of an optimal athletic nutrition program is to prevent glycogen depletion during exercise as much as possible and to restore glycogen stores in skeletal muscle and the liver as rapidly as possible after exercise. These goals can be accomplished by eating a high-energy, high carbohydrate diet during periods of intense training or competition and by consuming carbohydrate beverages during and after training.

Preventing Glycogen Depletion Glycogen depletion may be avoided to a certain extent by using fats as fuel during exercise. Using fats results in sparing muscle and liver glycogen stores. There are three ways to accomplish this:

1. Improve your ability to use fats
2. Mobilize fats early during exercise
3. Provide alternative fuels for the muscles, so that glycogen and blood sugar are not used up as rapidly

The best way to improve your ability to use fats is through endurance training. Endurance training increases the size of cellular structures called mitochondria, the cells' energy centers. Improved fat utilization is perhaps the most important benefit of over-distance endurance training. Although this type of training is used mostly by endurance athletes, it is also beneficial to body-builders because it improves the ability to control body fat.

Alternative fuels are important because their energy is available to your body sooner. You can use them as fuels sooner, thus sparing vital carbohydrate stores. A number of techniques have been used to increase fat mobilization, most notable is caffeine ingestion. The use of carbohydrate drinks during exercise has also been shown to be effective in sparing muscle and liver glycogen and maintaining blood sugar. But while caffeine ingestion prior to exercise and drinking carbohydrates during exercise have proven effective in endurance exercise, their effects on strength exercises are not completely understood. Caffeine (found in foods such as coffee, chocolate, and tea) causes nervousness and stomach upset in some people, so it cannot be universally recommended as a means of sparing glycogen during exercise.

The High Carbohydrate Diet The high carbohydrate diet is critical for active people involved in heavy training. This diet contains the seven basic food groups but emphasizes foods from the carbohydrate groups such as cereals, fruits, and grains. Numerous studies have shown that this diet enables athletes to exercise longer and more intensely and to recover faster than athletes on mixed or high protein–fat diets (Figure 8–1). Table 8–1 illustrates an example of a high energy, high carbohydrate diet that is appropriate for any athlete involved in intense training. This diet includes fresh vegetables for vitamins and minerals, meats and meat substitutes for protein and avoids refined sugar products such as cakes, pies, and candies. The consumption of alcoholic beverages should also be avoided or minimized.

Active people should take great care in designing their diets. It is important that enough calories and protein are consumed to optimize muscle growth; however, too much carbohydrate in the diet will result in a gain in body fat. A preliminary trial for any dietary change is a good idea to ensure that the diet is agreeable and palatable.

Carbohydrate Drinks During Exercise One of the most exciting findings in sports medicine research in recent years has been the discovery

Figure 8–1 *Effect of diet on performance*

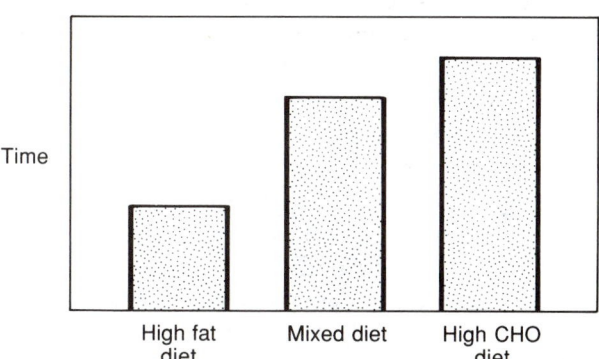

Table 8–1 Example of a Diet High in Energy and Carbohydrates

Breakfast

1 cup fruit juice (orange, grapefruit, guava)
Pancakes (2–3) with syrup
2 eggs
Ham, bacon, or sausage
Non-fat milk or hot chocolate

Lunch

Tuna salad sandwich
Fruit
Green salad
Non-fat milk

Dinner

Pasta with meat sauce (spaghetti, lasagna, etc.)
Bread
Green salad
Fruit
Non-fat milk

that consuming carbohydrate drinks during exercise improves performance. Drinks such as Max, Recharge, Gatorade, Isostar, and others maintain blood sugar levels during exercise and decrease the rate of glycogen breakdown in muscles and the liver. These effects substantially improve exercise performance and delay fatigue.

In addition, the use of carbohydrate drinks immediately after exercise results in a rapid replenishment of the glycogen that was used during exercise. Researchers have discovered that there is a two hour "window" immediately after exercise that is the optimal time for glycogen resynthesis. If a weight trainer consumes a carbohydrate drink during this two hour period after exercise, glycogen resynthesis in muscle and liver will be 20 percent greater than if a meal is eaten after that period. In other words, drinking a carbohydrate beverage immediately after exercise will allow you to come back sooner after a hard workout and will possibly prevent the feeling of fatigue that accompanies low glycogen levels in your body. Muscle and liver glycogen stores can be replenished to the maximum extent if, after exercise, you consume approximately .7–1.0 grams of glucose or sucrose per kilogram of body weight. A kilogram is equal to 2.2 pounds.

A word of caution about carbohydrate beverages.

> Never consume a carbohydrate drink   ◄ CAUTION
> before exercise (within 1–1½ hours).

Carbohydrates stimulate the release of insulin. Insulin moves sugar out of the blood and into the cells, which could cause low blood sugar during exercise. Carbohydrates are the most important fuels for the central nervous system and red blood cells. When carbohydrate levels in the blood are low, you feel sluggish, fatigued, and disoriented. Taking a drink high in sugar before exercise will backfire and decrease performance. It is all right to consume these drinks during and after exercise but not before exercise.

Avoiding High Fat Diets

Prior to 1965, a breakfast of bacon, eggs, and toast smothered in butter was almost a tradition in the United States. While still popular, many people avoid such meals because of the high fat and cholesterol content. Studies have shown that diets high in fat and cholesterol increase the risk of coronary heart disease (hardening of the arteries) and some types of cancer. Agencies such as the American Heart Association and the American Cancer Society recommend diets low in fat and cholesterol. A high carbohydrate diet will not only improve your physical performance but may also improve your health as well.

Protein Requirements of People on Weight Training Programs

Protein supplements have been popular among weight trainers for many years. However, most people who train with weights don't need any more protein than the average person. The daily protein requirement for active, healthy adults is approximately .8–1.0 grams per kilogram of body weight.

Several recent studies have suggested that athletes involved in extremely intense programs may have a higher protein requirement than average; however, this viewpoint is still controversial.

The protein requirements of the human body are determined by a complicated procedure called nitrogen balance. Proteins are composed of different combinations of amino acids. Amino acids contain nitrogen, and the nitrogen must be eliminated in order to use the amino acids as fuel. Nitrogen is an important marker of protein metabolism because its elimination from the body is directly proportional to the breakdown of amino acids. Protein breakdown in the body can be estimated by measuring nitrogen loss from the body in waste produces such as urine, feces, sweat, nail clippings, and hair loss. Protein intake can be estimated by measuring the quantity of nitrogen ingested in the diet. If the body is using more protein for fuel than is being taken in (a net loss of nitrogen), the person is said to be in a negative nitrogen balance. If, on the other hand, the person is incorporating more protein into body tissues than is being expended as fuel (a net gain in nitrogen), then the body is said to be in a positive nitrogen balance. The goal for people involved in a weight training program is to achieve a positive nitrogen balance. This means that the body is adding protein. In other words, a positive nitrogen balance suggests that the muscles are getting bigger and stronger, and in general, muscle strength is proportional to muscle size.

Nitrogen balance studies usually show that the vast majority of active people don't need additional protein in their diet. The average requirement of .8–1.0 grams of protein per kilogram of body weight is easily satisfied by the average American's diet. Nitrogen balance studies have shown that athletes who are involved in intense strength training (Olympic lifters, body-builders, football players, discus throwers, and so on) may have a protein requirement approaching 2.5 grams per kilogram per day, or several times that of the average active person. Extra protein is probably necessary only for elite or experienced weight-trained athletes involved in intense training. However, nutrition experts are not in agreement about the possible added protein requirements of athletes. Certainly, for people training at lower levels, protein supplements are unnecessary.

Proteins as an Energy Source Most energy released during exercise comes from carbohydrates and fats. Proteins can also be used for energy and play an important role in maintaining blood sugar through a process called gluconeogenesis (the formation of new blood sugar in the liver). Maintenance of blood sugar level during exercise is critical for maintaining exercise intensity. Low blood sugar causes fatigue, sluggishness, and disorientation. Proteins and amino acids help maintain blood sugar during exercise.

Because of its effect on blood sugar and metabolic regulation, the pregame or prepractice meal should contain some protein. For many years, physicians treating people with diabetes mellitus (a disease related to faulty blood sugar regulation) have recommended a diet with a significant protein component because the amino acids are very effective in assuring long-lasting release of sugar into the blood. In essence, the amino acids act like blood glucose releasing capsules.

Amino Acid and Polypeptide Supplements Amino acid and polypeptide supplements have been hailed as "natural" anabolic steroids that accelerate muscle development, decrease body fat, and stimulate the release of the growth hormone. Amino acids are the basic building blocks of proteins, and polypeptides are combinations of two or more amino acids linked together. Proponents of the use of amino acid and polypeptide supplements point to the more rapid absorption of the molecules as evidence of their superiority over normal dietary sources of protein.

Presently, there is little scientific evidence to support the need for amino acid or polypeptide supplementation in most active people. The rate of protein turnover in the muscle tissue of recreational weight trainers is not great enough to be affected by the rate of amino acid absorption from the gastrointestinal tract. Consequently, these supplements are a waste of money for most people.

There is some indirect evidence that amino acid or polypeptide supplements may be beneficial in elite weight-trained athletes. Muscle hypertrophy (enlargement) depends on the concentration of amino acids in the muscle—the more amino acids available, the faster the rate of muscle hypertrophy. Several studies have shown that elite weight-trained athletes often don't consume enough protein. In addition, when large amounts of protein are consumed, the rate of muscle hypertrophy accelerates. It may be that amino acid supplements provide a more readily available amino acid source for athletes with a high rate of muscle breakdown and growth, but presently, no data substantiates this hypothesis. However, it is clear that amino acid supplementation is of little use to the average recreational weight trainer.

Use of these supplements involves risks. Consuming an unbalanced amino acid formula (one that is high in some amino acids and deficient in others) has been shown to cause a negative nitrogen balance (a net loss of protein from the body). In addition, substituting amino acid or polypeptide supplements for protein rich foods may cause deficiencies in essential nutrients such as iron and the B vitamins. So, unless you are an elite athlete, stick to a well-balanced diet.

Other Nutritional Supplements

Although it is difficult to improve upon the balanced diet, various nutritional supplements have been investigated as possible ergogenic aids, substances or techniques that improve performance (Table 8–2). Possible nutritional ergogenic aids that have been studied recently include medium chain triglycerides, L-carnatine, succinates, and pyridoxine-alpha-ketoglutarate. The results of research studies on these substances have been contradictory. While some studies have shown that each of these substances may improve performance, other studies have shown no effect. Presently, it is not appropriate to recommend supplements of these substances to active individuals.

ANABOLIC STEROIDS

Anabolic steroids are drugs that resemble the male hormone testosterone. These drugs have been formulated to enhance the anabolic, or tissue building, effects of male hormones while minimizing their androgenic, or masculinizing, effects. Testosterone is produced mainly in the testes, but it and several related hormones are also produced in both the male and female adrenal glands. Testosterone is important in the development of primary and secondary sexual characteristics including development of the sex organs, facial hair, aggressiveness, and skeletal muscle growth.

Athletes take anabolic steroids in the hope of gaining weight and increasing strength, power, speed, endurance, and aggressiveness. They are widely used by athletes involved in track and field (mostly throwing) events, body building, weight lifting, and American football. A particularly disturbing trend is anabolic steroid use by nonathletic high school students hoping to increase their sex appeal. Many people who take these drugs are unaware of the risks involved. The use of these dangerous substances usually occurs without medical supervision. There have been numerous reports of serious illness or death attributable to the use of anabolic steroids. Consequently, unless they are prescribed by a physician, their use is illegal.

The first studies of the effects of male hormones on human physiology appeared in the 1930s. At that time, testosterone was isolated from the testes, and a technique was developed for producing it in the laboratory. To increase the length of time over which the drug worked, the testosterone molecule was modified, which resulted in drugs that were either injected or taken orally. Both modifications of the drug permitted large amounts of the male hormone to reach the target organs.

The first athletes reported to use anabolic steroids were soccer players of the 1939 Wolverhampton Wanderers team. During World War II, some German soldiers were given these hormones in an attempt to increase their aggressiveness. Gradually, the use of male hormones filtered into the world of sports, and by the 1960s, the use of anabolic steroids was relatively widespread. There are, however, a number of legitimate medical uses for testosterone and anabolic steroids. These include hormone replacement therapy for men with low testosterone output, stimulation of bone marrow (production of red blood cells) in patients with certain types of anemia (low blood count), malnutrition, osteoporosis (loss of bone mineral), depressed growth in children, and preoperative strengthening.

Scores of studies and articles have described the effects of these drugs on patients and athletes. Unfortunately, the research findings have been extremely inconsistent, some studies showing substantial gains in performance and others showing no effect. In 1978, the American College of Sports Medicine, summarizing the effects of the published studies on anabolic steroids, issued a position statement regarding the use and abuse of anabolic steroids. They stated that studies of the effects of anabolic steroids on athletic performance are contradictory and that, for many individuals, benefits are likely to be small and not worth the health risks involved.

The Effects of Anabolic Steroids on Health

While anabolic steroids may increase muscle size and strength in some people, they are potentially dangerous substances that can have severe side effects. Reported side effects of the drugs are summarized in Table 8–3. The available evidence suggests that although anabolic steroids may improve athletic performance, the benefits are not worth the health risks. Although most athletes do not experience serious short-term side effects (provided the dosage is moderate), severe effects including death have

Table 8–2 Some Substances Used as Ergogenic Aids

Alcohol
Amphetamines
Anabolic steroids
Aspartates
Bee pollen
Beta blockers
Caffeine
Cocaine
Cold
Digitalis
Electrical stimulation
Ephedrine
Epinephrine
Glucose
Growth hormone
Heat
Human chorionic gonadotropin
Hypnosis

(continued)

been reported among athletes taking anabolic steroids. The long-term consequences of anabolic steroid use in healthy athletes are not completely understood. Anabolic steroids use may result in coronary heart disease and liver cancer, but these conditions may take many years to develop. An athlete who doesn't experience any side effects from the drugs early on may be setting the stage for serious disease in later life. In general, the severity of steroid side effects seems to be affected by the dosage and duration of drug therapy. Athletes taking anabolic steroids may be taking an unnecessary chance.

Anabolic Steroid Use by Female Athletes The use of anabolic steroids by women has been reported in athletes involved in swimming, track and field, and body building. Women can expect relatively greater gains than

Table 8–2 (continued)
Inosine
Insulin
Lactate
Marijuana
Massage
Medium chain triglycerides
Negatively ionized air
Nicotine
Nitroglycerine
Norepinephrine
Oxygen
Protein supplements
Pyridoxine-alpha-ketoglutarate
Sodium bicarbonate
Strychnine
Succinates
Sulfa drugs
Vitamins
Wheat germ oil
Yeast

men can from anabolic steroid use, because the normal levels of male hormones circulating in a female's blood is low. However, the side effects are much more severe. In addition to the masculine changes already mentioned (male sexual characteristics), women on steroids typically experience acne, changes in skin texture, severe fluid retention, unnatural increases in muscle mass, and radically altered cholesterol metabolism. Women may also experience clitoral enlargement and menstrual irregularity. Many of these changes are irreversible, and the effects on fertility are unknown.

Anabolic Steroid Use by Children Children initially experience accelerated maturation followed by premature closure of the epiphyseal growth centers in the long bones. If anabolic steroid use is begun early in adolescence, the ultimate height of the individual may be compromised. Experts suspect that some young female gymnasts have used anabolic steroids in an effort to stunt growth because small stature is considered an advantage in women's gymnastics.

Effects of Anabolic Steroids on the Male Hormone Control System

Anabolic steroids have been shown to affect the regulation of the male hormone control system, resulting in a decreased production of testosterone by the testes. The suppression of testosterone can result in testicular atrophy and decreased sperm production.

Testosterone (or some synthetic anabolic steroids) is converted into estrogen. Excesses may result in gynecomastia, the development of female-like breast tissue in males. Approximately 20 percent of athletes who take steroids will develop gynecomastia. This condition will probably cause embarrassment to the athlete, and the long-term effects are not known. A recent report by the news media described an athlete on steroids who has developed breast cancer, but whether or not the steroids caused the condition is unknown.

Anabolic Steroids and the Immune System Anabolic steroids may also impair the immune system. Anabolic steroids also cause an increase in the production of other hormones called corticosteroids. Corticosteroids are known to suppress the immune system, and athletes will often suffer from colds or flu when going off steroids because of the surge in corticosteroid production.

Toxic Side Effects Oral anabolic steroids such as methandrostenolone (Dianabol) present the greatest risk of biological toxicity, particularly to the liver, because their structure has been altered to make them more biologically active. The steroid concentrates in the liver much earlier and in greater quantity than in the case of the injectable varieties. Athletes using anabolic steroids typically exhibit elevated blood levels of liver enzymes such as glutamic-oxalacetic transaminase (SGOT), glutamic-pyruvic transaminase (SGPT), and alkaline phosphatase, any of which suggest liver toxicity. Elevated levels of blood glucose, creatine kinase, and bilirubin have also been reported. These changes are usually reversible on withdrawal from the drug. Prolonged administration in some groups of individuals has been linked to severe liver disorders such as peliosis hepatitis (blood-filled cysts in the liver), hepatocellular carcinoma (liver cancer), and cholestasis (bile duct obstruction). Several cases of suspected

Table 8–3 Reported Side Effects of Anabolic Steroids

- ▶ Abnormal bleeding and blood clotting
- ▶ Acne
- ▶ Breast enlargement in males
- ▶ Decreased male hormone levels
- ▶ Depressed sperm production
- ▶ Dizziness
- ▶ Elevated blood pressure
- ▶ Elevated blood sugar
- ▶ Gastrointestinal distress
- ▶ Heart disease
- ▶ Impaired immune function
- ▶ Increased aggressiveness
- ▶ Liver cancer
- ▶ Liver toxicity
- ▶ Masculinization in women and children
- ▶ Prostatic cancer
- ▶ Stunted growth in children
- ▶ Tissue swelling

anabolic steroid–linked cancer cases in athletes have been reported in the medical literature and news media.

Anabolic Steroids and Heart Disease A particularly disturbing observation in athletes taking anabolic steroids is an apparent increase in the probability of developing coronary artery disease. These athletes often have high levels of cholesterol and triglycerides, elevated blood pressure, and decreased levels of high density lipoproteins. (High levels of HDL are thought to provide protection against coronary heart disease.) Many weight-trained athletes compete from ten to more than twenty years, subjecting themselves to the real possibility of premature death from heart disease and stroke. Hypertension (high blood pressure) is also common, probably due to the fluid retention properties of these drugs.

Miscellaneous Side Effects A variety of miscellaneous side effects to anabolic steroids has been reported including muscle cramps, gastrointestinal distress, headache, dizziness, sore nipples, and abnormal thyroid function. Some of these side effects have become manifest even in individuals who took low doses for short periods of time. To summarize, anabolic steroids are probably effective for increasing strength and lean body mass in trained athletes, but they present possible grave health risks that could be life-threatening.

DEVELOPING AN ATTRACTIVE BODY

Perhaps the most important reason for the tremendous popularity of weight training among men and women is the way the activity improves physical appearance. People who train with weights look more athletic, tighter, and muscular than other people. Paradoxically, some people use weight training to help them gain weight while others use it to lose weight. This concept is possible to understand if you first understand the principle of energy balance as it applies to body composition.

Weight Training, Energy Balance, and Body Composition

All of the energy absorbed must be accounted for as energy used in body functions, energy stored as fat, or energy lost as heat. This is a basic law of nature, and there is no other place for food energy to go. If more energy is taken in than is needed, then body fat increases. If less energy is taken in than required, then fat is lost.

It is difficult to significantly affect energy balance through weight training because the activity requires relatively few calories (compared to activities such as long-distance running). Contrary to popular belief, you cannot spot reduce—exercise a particular body part so that fat will be reduced in that area. Studies have shown that spot reducing doesn't result from exercise. Weight training can, however, have a tremendous effect on physical appearance, even if body fat is unaltered.

Body composition can be segmented into fat and fat-free weight. Fat-free or lean body weight is largely composed of muscle. Strengthening a body part, such as the abdominal muscles, increases muscle tone and "tightens up" the area. Strong abdominal muscles are less likely to sag, and the area looks more attractive. Unfortunately, excess fat still remains, but it looks better. Weight training can play an important role in helping people gain or lose weight or simply be more attractive if it is practiced as part of a comprehensive diet and exercise program.

Scientists have developed a classification system for describing body types. You are limited in your ability to change the appearance of your body by your body type, or somatotype. Three basic somatotypes have been identified: ectomorphs, endomorphs, and mesomorphs. Ectomorphs tend to be very linear, slim people. Endomorphs tend to be rounder people with more body fat. Mesomorphs are muscular, athletic-looking people. Most people tend to be combinations of the three types, with one somatotype predominating in each person. You can change your body composition to a certain extent, but you are limited in your ability to change your basic appearance by your somatotype.

Gaining Weight Many people are naturally underweight and seek to gain weight. Others, such as football players and throwers, are participating in sports where increased body mass is an advantage. The two basic ways to increase body weight are to increase muscle or fat. While many lean people can increase body fat with little or no adverse effect on appearance or health, they should strive to gain "quality weight." This can be accomplished only through a vigorous weight training program that stresses the large muscle groups in the legs, hips, shoulders, arms, and chest. Muscle weight takes many years to gain but is certainly preferable to the fat that is quickly gained from extensive high-calorie weight gain supplements or unhealthy high-fat diets. Some basic guidelines for gaining weight include:

- ▶ Stress quality over quantity in body weight. Carrying extra fat does little to improve physical performance or appearance.
- ▶ Use weight training to increase the size of major muscle groups. Stress exercises that work large muscle groups. Exercises should consist principally of presses (for example, bench press and seated press) and high resistance leg exercises (for example, squats and leg presses). Lifts should employ heavy resistance and numerous sets (for example, five sets of five repetitions).
- ▶ Stress long-term gains. Do not expect to increase lean body mass by more than 8–10 lbs per year.
- ▶ Don't use drugs to gain weight. Avoid drugs such as anabolic steroids and growth hormone. The benefits are not worth the risks.

- ▶ Eat a regular, well-balanced diet containing slightly more calories than normal. If you are training vigorously, your protein requirement may increase slightly to 1.0–1.5 grams per kilogram body weight (1 kilogram is 2.2 lbs).

- ▶ Monitor your body composition. Keep track of your progress by measuring your lean body mass and body fat. The underwater weighing technique is the most accurate. This test is performed in many college and university physical education departments, sports medicine centers, and health clubs. The skin fold and electrical impedance techniques of body composition measurement are also widely available and are reasonably accurate. Ask your weight training instructor or coach for further information.

- ▶ Consult a physician if you do not make progress. There are several explanations for being chronically underweight including family history, maturational level, or metabolic status.

Losing Weight Weight loss is a national obsession. Many people train with weights or participate in other forms of physical activity in the hope of keeping their waistline under control. We've learned that the body's energy balance determines whether body fat increases, decreases, or remains the same. Fat gains occur when more energy (food) is consumed than expended by the body. While exercise is an important part of a weight control program, caloric restriction is essential if the program is to be successful.

The goal of a weight control program should be to lose body fat and maintain the loss. Quick-loss programs often result in the loss of muscle tissue and do nothing to instill healthy, long-term dietary habits that will help you maintain the new weight. Here are five principles for losing body fat that will increase the chances of success in the weight control program:

- ▶ Stress fat loss rather than weight loss. Rapid weight loss from fad diets is often caused by the loss of muscle mass and water. Therefore, fat loss rather than weight loss should be the goal.

- ▶ Restrict the amount of weight you lose. Lose no more than 1½–2 lbs per week. More rapid weight loss results in the loss of muscle tissue.

- ▶ Eat a balanced diet that is relatively high in complex carbohydrates and low in fat. Create a caloric deficit by combining caloric restriction with more exercise.

- ▶ Exercise, particularly endurance exercise, is critical to a successful weight loss program. The best exercises for losing weight are running, walking, and cycling.

▶ Monitor your body composition. Make sure that most of the weight loss is from a reduction in body fat rather than a reduction in lean body mass.

References

Anabolic Steroids and Other Ergogenic Aids

Aakvaag, A. and S.B. Stromme. The effect of mesterolone administration to normal men on the pituitary–testicular function. *Acta Endocrinol.* 77:380–386, 1974.

Alen, M., K. Hakkinen, and P.V. Komi. Changes in neuromuscular performance and muscle fiber characteristics of elite power athletes self administering androgenic and anabolic steroids. *Acta Physiol. Scand.* 122:535–544, 1984.

Ariel, G. and W. Saville. Anabolic steroids: The physiological effects of placebo. *Med. Sci. Sports* 4:124–126, 1972.

Brooks, G.A. Amino acid and protein metabolism during exercise and recovery. *Med. Sci. Sports Exerc.* 19(Suppl.):150–156, 1987.

Castner, S., R. Early, and B.R. Carlton. Anabolic steroid effects on body composition in normal young men. *J. Sports Med. Phys. Fitness* 11:98–103, 1971.

Crist, D.M., P.J. Stackpole, and G.T. Peake. Effects of androgenic–anabolic steroids on neuromuscular power and body composition. *J. Appl. Physiol.* 54:366–370, 1983.

Fahey, T.D. and C.H. Brown. The effects of an anabolic steroid on the strength, body composition, and endurance of college males when accompanied by a weight training program. *Med. Sci. Sport* 5:272–276, 1973.

Fowler, W.M., G.W. Gardner, and G.H. Egstrom. Effect of an anabolic steroid on the physical performance of young men. *J. Appl. Physiol.* 20:1038–1040, 1965.

Frankle, M.A., G.J. Cicero, and J. Payne. Use of androgenic anabolic steroids by athletes. *JAMA* 252:482, 1984.

Freed, D.L.J., A.J. Banks, D. Longson, and D.M. Burley. Anabolic steroids in athletics: Crossover double-blind trial in weight-lifters. *Brit. Med. J.* 2:471–473, 1975.

Haupt, H.A. and G.D. Rovere. Anabolic steroids: A review of the literature. *Am. J. Sports Med.* 12:469–484, 1984.

Hervey, G.R., A.V. Knibbs, L. Burkinshaw, D.B. Morgan, P.R.M. Jones, D.R. Chettle, and D.R. Vartsky. Effects of methandienone on the performance and body composition of men undergoing athletic training. *Clin. Sci.* 60:457–461, 1981.

Holma, P. Effects of anabolic steroid (metandienone) on spermatogenesis. *Contraception* 15:151–162, 1977.

Johnson, L.C., G. Fisher, L.J. Sylvester, and C.C. Hofheins. Anabolic steroid: Effects on strength, body weight, oxygen uptake and spermatogenesis upon mature males. *Med. Sci. Sports* 4:43–45, 1972.

Kochakian, C.D. (Ed.) *Anabolic–androgenic Steroids.* Berlin, W. Germany: Springer–Verlag, 1976.

Lamb, D.R. Anabolic steroids in athletics: How well do they work and how dangerous are they? *Amer. J. Sports Med.* 12:31–38, 1987.

Lamb, D.R. Androgens and exercise. *Med. Sci. Sports* 7:1–5, 1975.

Ljungqvist, A. The use of anabolic steroids in top Swedish athletes. *Br. J. Sports Med.* 9:82, 1975.

Marconi, C., G. Sassi, and P. Ceretelli. The effect of alpha–ketoglutarate-pyrodoxine complex on human maximal aerobic and anaerobic performance. *Eur. J. Appl. Physiol.* 49:307–317, 1982.

Marconi, C., G. Sassi, A. Carpinelli, and P. Ceretelli. Effects of L–carnitine loading on the aerobic and anaerobic performance of endurance athletes. *Eur. J. Appl. Physiol.* 54:131–135, 1985.

Merkin, G. Carbohydrate loading: A dangerous practice. *J. Am. Med. Assoc.* 223:1511–1512, 1973.

Meyers, F.H., E. Jawetz, and A. Goldfien. *Review of Medical Pharmacology.* Los Altos, Ca.: Lang Medical Pub., 1980.

Morgan, W. (Ed.) *Ergogenic Aids and Muscular Performance.* New York, NY: Academic Press, 1972.

Peterson, G.E. and T.D. Fahey. HDL–C in five elite athletes using anabolic-androgenic steroids. *Physician Sportsmed.* 12(6):120–130, 1984.

Rich, V. Drugs in athletics: Mortality of Soviet athletes. *Nature* 311:402–403, 1984.

Shephard, R.J., D. Killinger, and T. Fried. Response to sustained use of anabolic steroid. *Brit. J. Sports Med.* 11:170–173, 1977.

Souccar, C., A.J. Lapa, and R.B. doValle. The influence of testosterone on neuromuscular transmission in hormone sensitive mammalian skeletal muscles. *Muscle and Nerve* 5:232–237, 1982.

Strauss, R.H., J.E. Wright, and G.A.M. Finerman. Anabolic steroid use and health status among forty-two weight-trained male athletes. *Med. Sci. Sports* 14:119, 1982.

Strauss, R.H., J.E. Wright, G.A.M. Finerman, and D.H. Catlin. Side-effects of anabolic steroids in weight-trained men. *Physician and Sports Med.* 11:87–96, 1983.

Taylor, W.N. *Anabolic Steroids and the Athlete.* Jefferson, NC: McFarland & Co., 1982.

Williams, M.H. *Drugs and Athletic Performance.* Springfield, Il.: Charles C. Thomas, 1974.

Williams, M.H. (Ed.) *Ergogenic Aids in Sport.* Champaign, Il.: Human Kinetics Publishers, 1983.

Wright, J. *Anabolic Steroids and Sports.* Natick, Ma.: Sports Science Consultants, 1978.

Wright, J. *Anabolic Steroids and Sports, Vol. 2.* Natick, Ma.: Sports Science Consultants, 1982.

Wright, J. Anabolic steroids and athletics. *Exercise and Sports Science Reviews* 8:149–202, 1980.

Nutrition

Ahlborg, G. and P. Felig. Influence of glucose ingestion on fuel–hormone response during prolonged exercise. *J. Appl. Physiol.* 41:683–688, 1976.

American Association for Health, Physical Education, and Recreation. *Nutrition for the Athlete.* Washington DC: AAHPER, 1971.

Bach, A.C. and V.K. Babayan. Medium–chain triglycerides: An update. *Am. J. Clin. Nutr.* 36:950–962, 1982.

Belko, A.Z. Vitamins and exercise—an update. *Med. Sci. Sports Exerc.* 19(Suppl.):191–196, 1987.

Bergstrom, J., L. Hermansen, E. Hultman, and B. Saltin. Diet, muscle glycogen and physical performance. *Acta Physiol. Scand.* 71:140–150, 1967.

Bergstrom, J. and E. Hultman. A study of the glycogen metabolism during exercise in man. *Scand. J. Clin. Lab. Invest.* 19:218–228, 1967.

Bergstrom, J. and E. Hultman. Nutrition for maximal sports performance. *J. Am. Med. Assoc.* 221:999–1006, 1972.

Bergstrom, J. and E. Hultman. Synthesis of muscle glycogen in man after glucose and fructose infusion. *Acta Med. Scand.* 182:93–107, 1967.

Blom, P.C.S., A.T. Hostmark, O. Vaage, K.R. Kardel, and S. Maehlum. Effect of different post-exercise sugar diets on the rate of muscle glycogen synthesis. *Med. Sci. Sports Exerc.* 19:491–496, 1987.

Brooks, G.A. Amino acid and protein metabolism during exercise and recovery. *Med. Sci. Sports Exerc.* 19(Suppl):150–156, 1987.

Brooks, G.A. and T.D. Fahey. *Exercise Physiology: Human Bioenergetics and its Applications.* New York, NY: Macmillan, 1984.

Brooks, G.A. and T.D. Fahey. *Fundamentals of Human Performance.* New York, NY: Macmillan, 1987.

Buskirk, E.R. Diet and athletic performance. *Postgrad. Med.* 61:229–236, 1977.

Buskirk, E.R. Some nutritional considerations in the conditioning of athletes. *Ann. Rev. Nutr.* 1:319–350, 1981.

Butterfield, G. and D. Calloway. Physical activity improves protein utilization in young men. *Br. J. Nutr.* 51:171–184, 1984.

Buzina, K., R. Buzina, G. Brubacker, J. Sapunar, and S. Christeller. Vitamin C status and physical working capacity in adolescents. In: *J. Vit. Nutr. Res.* 54:55–60, 1984.

Celejowa, I. and M. Homa. Food intake, nitrogen and energy balance in Polish weight lifters during a training camp. *Nutrition and Metabolism* 12:259–274, 1970.

Consolazio, C.F., H.L. Johnson, R.A. Dramise, and J.A. Skata. Protein metabolism during intensive physical training in the young adult. *Am. J. Clin. Nutr.* 28:29–35, 1975.

Costill, D.L. and B. Saltin. Factors limiting gastric emptying during rest and exercise. *J. Appl. Physiol.* 37:679–683, 1974.

Costill, D.L., A. Bennett, G. Brahnam, and D. Eddy. Glucose ingestion at rest and during prolonged severe exercise. *J. Appl. Physiol.* 34:764–769, 1973.

Costill, D.L. and J.M. Miller. Nutrition for endurance sport: Carbohydrate and fluid balance. *Int. J. Sports Med.* 1:2–14, 1980.

Dragan, G.I.A., A. Vasiliu, and E. Georgescu. Effect of increased supply of protein on elite weight–lifters. In: *Milk Proteins.* T.E. Galesloot and B.J. Tinbergen (Eds.) Wageningen, The Netherlands: Prodoc, 1985, p.99–103.

Durnin, J.V.G.A. Protein requirements and physical activity. In: J. Parizkova and V.A. Rogozkin (Eds.) *Nutrition, Physical Fitness and Health.* Baltimore, Md.: University Press, 1978, 53–60.

Fahey, T.D. (Ed.) *Athletic Training: Principles and Practice.* Mountain View, Ca.: Mayfield Publishing, 1986.

Foster, C., D.L. Costill, and W.J. Fink. Effects of pre-exercise feedings on endurance performance. *Med. Sci. Sports* 11:1–5, 1979.

Geliebter, A., E.F. Bracco, T.B. Van Itallie, and S.A. Hashim. Medium-chain triglyceride diet and obesity. *Int. J. Obesity* 8:191–192, 1984.

Gollnick, P.D., K. Piehl, I.V. Saubert, C.W. Armstrong, and B. Saltin. Diet, exercise, and glycogen changes in human muscle fibers. *J. Appl. Physiol.* 33:421–425, 1972.

Gontzea, I., R. Sutzescu, and S. Dumitrache. The influence of adaptation to physical effort on nitrogen balance in man. *Nutr. Rep. Int.* 11:231–236, 1975.

Haskell, W., J. Scala, and J. Whittam (Eds.). *Nutrition and Athletic Performance.* Palo Alto, Ca.: Bull Publishing Co., 1982.

Haymes, E.M. Nutritional concerns: Needs for iron. *Med. Sci. Sports Exerc.* 19(Suppl.):197–200, 1987.

Hickson, R.C., M.J. Rennie, W.W. Winder, and J.O. Holloszy. Effects of increased plasma fatty acids on glycogen utilization and endurance. *J. Appl. Physiol.* 43:829–833, 1977.

Ivy, J.L., D.L. Costill, W.J. Fink, and E. Maglischo. Contribution of medium and long chain triglyceride intake to energy metabolism during prolonged exercise. *Int. J. Sports Med.* 1:15–20, 1980.

Jansson, E. Diet and muscle metabolism in man. *Acta Physiol. Scand.* (Supp.)487:1–24, 1980.

Jette, M., O. Pelletier, L. Parker, and J. Thoden. The nutritional and metabolic effects of a carbohydrate-rich diet in a glycogen supracompensation training regimen. *Am. J. Clin. Nutr.* 31:2140–2148, 1978.

Johnson, C.C., M.H. Stone, R.J. Byrd, and S.A. Lopez. The response of serum lipids and plasma androgens to weight training exercise in sedentary males. *J. Sports Med.* 23:39–44, 1983.

Karlsson, J. and B. Saltin. Diet, muscle glycogen, and endurance performance. *J. Appl. Physiol.* 31:203–206, 1971.

Laritcheva, K., N. Yalovaya, P. Smirnov, V. Schubin, V. Belaev, and M. Kim. Protein needs of highly qualified weight–lifters. *Tyach. Atlet.* 32–33, 1978.

Lemon, P.W.R. Protein and exercise: Update 1987. *Med. Sci. Sports Exerc.* 19(Suppl.):179–190, 1987.

Lemon, P.W.R. and J.P. Mullin. Effect of initial muscle glycogen levels on protein catabolism during exercise. *J. Appl. Physiol.* 48:624–629, 1980.

Matthews, D.M. and S.A. Adibi. Peptide absorption. *Gastroenterology* 71:151–161, 1976.

Pate, R.R., M. Maguire, and J. Van Wyk. Dietary iron supplementation in women atheltes. *Physician and Sportsmed.* 7:81–101, 1979.

Senior, J.R. (Ed.) *Medium Chain Triglycerides.* Philadelphia, Pa.: University of Pennsylvania Press, 1968.

Sherman, W.M., M.J. Plyley, R.L. Sharp, P.J. Van Handle, R.M. McAllister, W.J. Fink, and D.L. Costill. Muscle glycogen storage and its relationship to water. *Int. J. Sports Med.* 3:22–24, 1982.

Smith, N. Nutrition and athletic performance. *Medical Times* 109:91–107, 1981.

Smith, N.J. *Food for Sport.* Palo Alto, Ca.: Bull Publishing Co., 1976.

Whereeat, A.F., F.E. Hull, M.W. Orishimo, and J.L. Rabinowitz. The role of succinate in the regulation of fatty acid synthesis by heart mitochondria. *J. Biological Chem.* 242:4013–4022, 1967.

Williams, M.H. *Nutritional Aspects of Human Physical and Athletic Performance.* Springfield, Il.: Charles C. Thomas, 1988.

Young, D.R. *Physical Performance, Fitness, and Diet.* Springfield, Il.: Charles C. Thomas, 1977.

▼

Muscular System

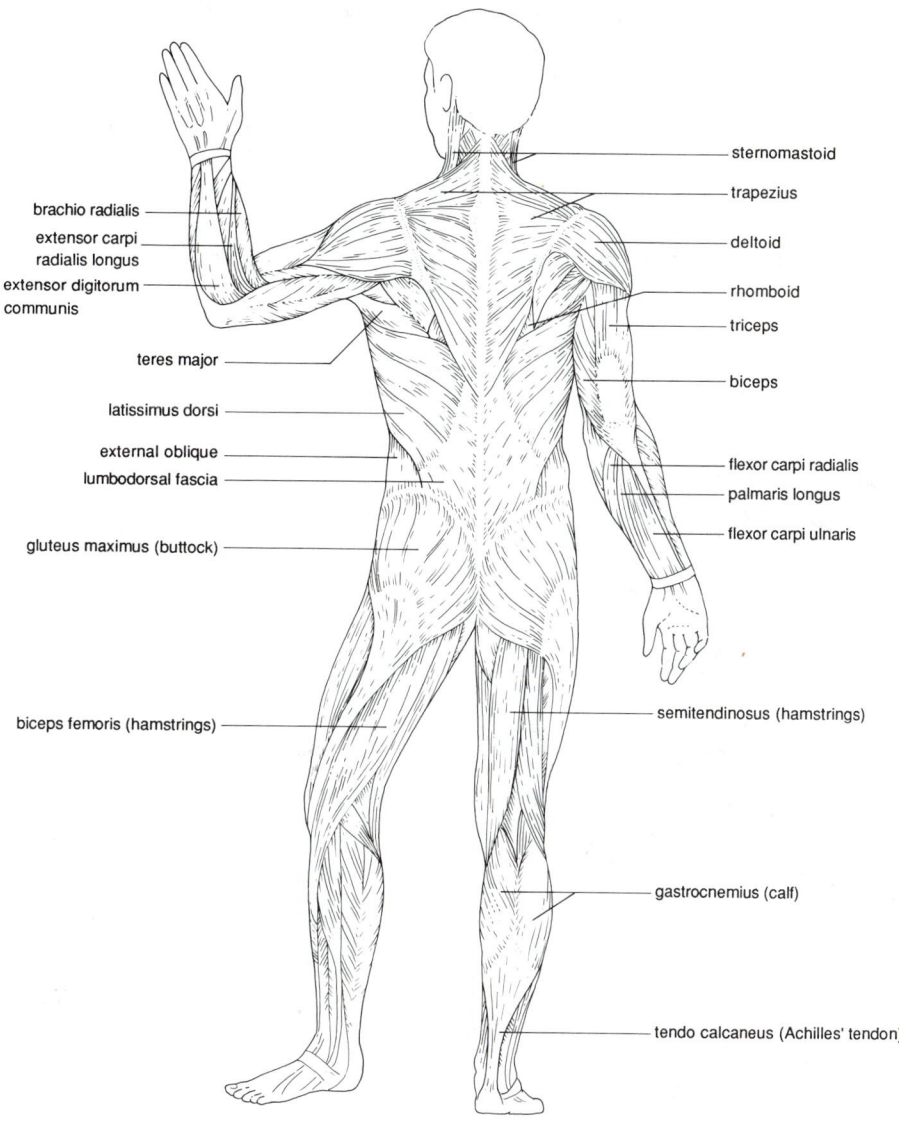

- brachio radialis
- extensor carpi radialis longus
- extensor digitorum communis
- teres major
- latissimus dorsi
- external oblique
- lumbodorsal fascia
- gluteus maximus (buttock)
- biceps femoris (hamstrings)
- sternomastoid
- trapezius
- deltoid
- rhomboid
- triceps
- biceps
- flexor carpi radialis
- palmaris longus
- flexor carpi ulnaris
- semitendinosus (hamstrings)
- gastrocnemius (calf)
- tendo calcaneus (Achilles' tendon)

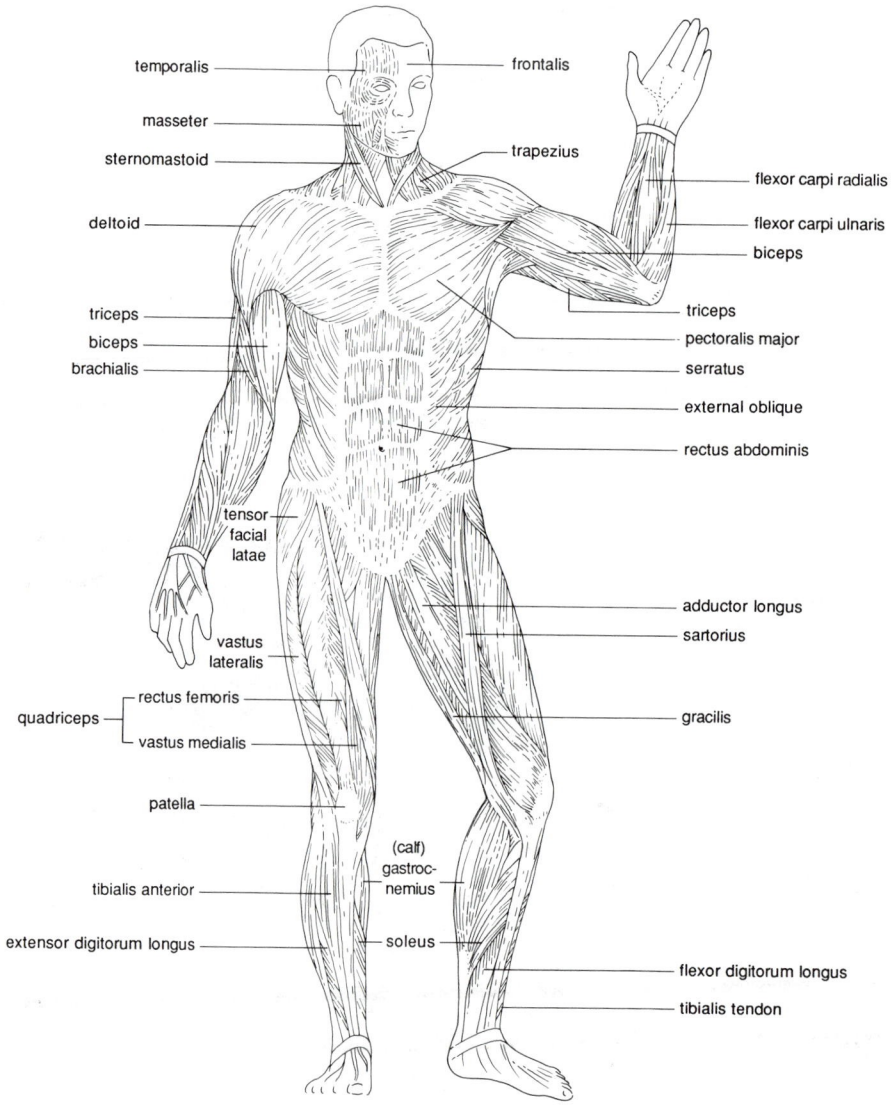

temporalis — frontalis

masseter

sternomastoid — trapezius

deltoid — flexor carpi radialis

flexor carpi ulnaris

biceps

triceps — triceps

biceps — pectoralis major

brachialis — serratus

external oblique

rectus abdominis

tensor facial latae

adductor longus

sartorius

vastus lateralis

rectus femoris

quadriceps

vastus medialis — gracilis

patella

(calf) gastrocnemius

tibialis anterior

extensor digitorum longus — soleus

flexor digitorum longus

tibialis tendon

▼

Sample Weight Programs to Build Strength for Sports

GENERAL PROGRAM

- ▶ Train with weights three days per week (no less than two).
- ▶ Participate in aerobic (endurance) exercise 3–5 days per week. Good aerobic exercises include walking, jogging, swimming, and cycling. Start-and-stop sports such as tennis, racquetball, and basketball are acceptable if the intensity of play is vigorous.
- ▶ Do flexibility (stretching) exercises for your major muscle groups at least five days per week. All stretching should be done statically (don't bounce). Stretch the muscle until you feel tightness without pain. Hold the stretch for 15–60 seconds.

Example of General Weight Training Program

Exercise	Sets	Repetitions
Bench press	3	10
Lat pulls	3	10
Lateral raises	3	10
Biceps curls	3	10
Triceps extensions	3	10
Abdominal curls	3	10
Squats	3	10
Calf raises	3	10

CONDITIONING FOR ALPINE SKIING

▶ Participate in aerobic exercise 3–5 times per week. Running, cross-country skiing, and cycling are probably the best forms of endurance exercise for alpine skiers. Include some high intensity aerobics (fast running, fast cycling, and so on) in your program because skiing often requires rapid, powerful movements.

▶ Although total body conditioning is critical, concentrate on lower body exercises in the weight training program. In addition to leg exercises, do exercises for the back, abdominals, and shoulders.

▶ Stretch every day. Flexibility is extremely important for preventing injury and achieving optimal technique.

Sample Program for Alpine Skiers

Exercise	Sets	Repetitions
Lat pulls	3	10
Bench press	3	10
Triceps push-downs	3	10
Abdominal curls	3	25
Back extensions	3	15
Knee extensions	3	10
Knee flexions	3	10
Squats	3	10
Calf raises	3	10

CONDITIONING FOR TENNIS

▶ Tennis is largely an anaerobic activity (start-and-stop), but endurance is important and an adjunct running program is helpful for achieving optimal fitness for the sport. Try to run at least two days a week (in addition to playing tennis). Run fast at least one day a week. An example of a fast running workout is to sprint or stride the straight-a-ways of a 400-meter running track and walk the turns. On the other running days, jog 2–5 miles.

- ▶ Stretch at least five days a week. Important areas to stretch are the shoulders, thighs, hamstrings, and forearm extensor muscles.
- ▶ Weight training should stress general conditioning but should include exercises for the rotator cuff muscles of the shoulder and forearm extensor muscles. These additional exercises will help prevent injuries to the shoulder and elbow, which are extremely common in tennis players.

Sample Program for Tennis Players

Exercise	Sets	Repetitions
Bench press	3	10
Lat pulls	3	10
Biceps curls	3	10
Triceps extensions	3	10
Abdominal curls	3	10
Squats	3	10
Calf raises	3	10
Rotator cuff exercises	3	10
Empty can exercise	3	10
Wrist extensions	3	10

CONDITIONING FOR VOLLEYBALL

- ▶ Like tennis, volleyball is a start-and-stop activity requiring quickness, explosiveness, and endurance. Run at least two days a week to supplement endurance fitness. One of those days should include fast running and sprinting.
- ▶ Plyometric exercises (see Chapter 2) are helpful for improving your ability to jump. Do not do excessive amounts of plyometrics until you are well conditioned. Try to perform leg exercises explosively. This will improve the height of your jumps.
- ▶ Stretch regularly to help prevent injuries.
- ▶ Upper and lower body exercises are important for volleyball players. In addition to major muscle exercises for the legs and upper body, include exercises for the calves, rotator cuff (shoulders), and back.

Sample Program for Volleyball Players

Exercise	Sets	Repetitions
Bench press	3	10
Push-presses or jerks	3	10
Lat pulls	3	10
Biceps curls	3	10
Triceps extensions	3	10
Abdominal curls	3	10
Squats	3	10
Calf raises	3	10
Rotator cuff exercises	3	10
Empty can exercise	3	10

CONDITIONING FOR FOOTBALL

Football players are made during the off season. If August rolls around and you are not physically prepared for those dreaded two-a-days, it's too late. You have set yourself up for a miserable and difficult preseason and, perhaps, for an injury and a mediocre football season. With the proper conditioning program, you can report to the first day of practice as a strong, quick, flexible, and smart football player.

▶ Stay in good shape all year long.

▶ The most important weight lifting exercises for football players are presses, pulls, and squats. Work on areas of the body particularly susceptible to injury such as the neck and lower back.

▶ Do stretching exercises for the major muscle groups of the body, particularly the hamstrings, quadriceps, calves, and lower back.

▶ Run 3–6 days per week. Begin with jogging during the spring and progress to repeated sprints as the season nears. Remember that football is an explosive sport that requires fitness for high intensity exercise. Don't rely on slow jogs to get you into shape for football.

▶ Work on football skills. There is much more to being a good football player than merely being in good shape. You have to be able to play the game.

Example of a Weight Training Program for Beginning Football Players

Weights are for example only and will vary with the strength of the athlete.

Exercise	Sets	Repetitions	Weight (lbs)
Monday			
Bench press	6	6	170
Lat pulls	3	10	90
Squats	6	8	175
Power cleans	5	5	100
Neck exercises	3	10	20
Abdominal curls	3	20	—
Back extensions	3	15	—
Arm curls	3	10	60
Triceps extensions	3	10	35
Wednesday			
Incline press	3	10	100
Pull-ups	5	5	—
Pullovers	3	10	40
Leg press	3	10	290 (machine)
Calf raises	4	20	290 (machine)
Neck exercises	3	10	20
Abdominal curls	3	40	—
Good mornings	3	10	35
Friday			
Bench press	3	10	140
Power cleans	5	5	125
Lat pulls	3	10	110
Neck exercises	3	10	20
Squats	3	10	150
Abdominal curls	3	20	—
Back extensions	3	15	—
Arm curls	4	10	70
Triceps extensions	4	10	40

CONDITIONING FOR BASEBALL AND SOFTBALL

▶ Baseball and softball require powerful legs and hips because the muscle groups in these areas supply the power to hit the ball. Work on muscle groups susceptible to injury such as the rotator cuff (shoulder), hamstrings, quadriceps, and lower back.

▶ Do stretching exercises for the quadriceps, hamstrings, shoulders, and lower back.

▶ Run at least three days per week. During the off-season, begin with jogging, then progress to sprints.

Weight Training for Baseball and Softball

Exercise	Sets	Repetitions
Bench press	3	10
Lat pulls	3	10
Biceps curls	3	10
Hamstring curls	3	10
Triceps extensions	3	10
Abdominal curls	3	10
Squats	3	10
Calf raises	3	10
Rotator cuff exercises	3	10
Empty can exercise	3	10
Wrist extensions/ flexions	3	10
Back extensions	3	10

CONDITIONING FOR GOLF

▶ Golf requires lower body explosiveness, flexibility in the torso, and strong arms and shoulders.

- ▶ While golf does not require a high degree of aerobic fitness, it is important to be able to walk long distances without tiring. Walking is perhaps the best physical preparation for the sport. Try to walk at least three days a week for 45–60 minutes.
- ▶ Injuries to the back are relatively common among golfers. It is important to develop good strength and flexibility in the lower back. Work on flexibility of the back, hips, and shoulders every day.

Weight Training for Golfers

Exercise	Sets	Repetitions
Bench press	3	10
Lat pulls	3	10
Biceps curls	3	10
Triceps extensions	3	10
Abdominal curls	3	10
Twists	3	20
Squats	3	10
Wrist extensions/flexions	3	10
Back extensions	3	10
Isometric back exercise	3	10

References

Ahlborg, G. and P. Felig. Influence of glucose ingestion on fuel–hormone response during prolonged exercise. *J. Appl. Physiol.* 41:683–688, 1976.

Alen, M., K. Hakkinen, and P.V. Komi. Changes in neuromuscular performance and muscle fiber characteristics of elite power athletes self-administering androgenic and anabolic steroids. *Acta Physiol. Scand.* 122:535–544, 1984.

Alen, M. and P. Rahkila. Reduced high-density lipoprotein cholesterol in power athletes: Use of male sex hormone derivates, an atherogenic factor. *Int. J. Sports Med.* 5:341–342, 1984.

American Association for Health, Physical Education, and Recreation. *Nutrition for the Athlete.* Washington D.C.: AAHPER, 1971.

Ariel, G. and W. Saville. Anabolic steroids: The physiological effects of placebo. *Med. Sci. Sports* 4:124–126, 1972.

Armstrong, R.B. Mechanisms of exercise-induced delayed onset muscular soreness: A brief review. *Med. Sci. Sports Exerc.* 16:529–538, 1984.

Atha, J. Strengthening muscle. *Exercise and Sport Sciences Reviews* 9:1–73, 1981.

Belko, A.Z. Vitamins and exercise—an update. *Med. Sci. Sports Exerc.* 19(Suppl.):191–196, 1987.

Berger, R. Optimum repetitions for the development of strength. *Research Quarterly* 33:334–338, 1962.

Bergstrom, J. and E. Hultman. Muscle glycogen synthesis after exercise: An enhancing factor localized to the muscle cells in man. *Nature* 210:309–310, 1966.

Bergstrom, J. and E. Hultman. Nutrition for maximal sports performance. *J. Am. Med. Assoc.* 221:999–1006, 1972.

Bergstrom, J. and E. Hultman. A study of the glycogen metabolism during exercise in man. *Scand. J. Clin. Lab. Invest.* 19:218–228, 1967.

Bergstrom, J. and E. Hultman. Synthesis of muscle glycogen in man after glucose and fructose infusion. *Acta Med. Scand.* 182:93–107, 1967.

Bergstrom, J., L. Hermansen, E. Hultman, and B. Saltin. Diet, muscle glycogen and physical performance. *Acta Physiol. Scand.* 71:140–150, 1967.

Bowers, R. and J. Reardon. Effects of methandrostenolone (Dianabol) on strength development and aerobic capacity. *Med. Sci. Sports* 4:54, 1972.

Brooks, G.A. Amino acid and protein metabolism during exercise and recovery. *Med. Sci. Sports Exerc.* 19(Suppl.):150–156, 1987.

Brooks, G.A. and T.D. Fahey. *Exercise Physiology: Human Bioenergetics and Its Applications.* New York, NY: Macmillan, 1984.

Brooks, G.A. and T.D. Fahey. *Fundamentals of Human Performance.* New York, NY: Macmillan, 1987.

Buskirk, E.R. Diet and athletic performance. *Postgrad. Med.* 61:229–236, 1977.

Buskirk, E.R. Some nutritional considerations in the conditioning of athletes. *Ann. Rev. Nutr.* 1:319–350, 1981.

Butterfield, G. and D. Calloway. Physical activity improves protein utilization in young men. *Br. J. Nutr.* 51:171–184, 1984.

Buzina, K., R. Buzina, G. Brubacker, J. Sapunar, and S. Christeller. Vitamin C status and physical working capacity in adolescents. *In: J. Vit. Nutr. Res.* 54:55–60, 1984.

Carlin, J.I., W.G. Redden, M. Sanjak, and R. Hodack. Carnitine metabolism during prolonged exercise and recovery in humans. *J. Appl. Physiol.* 61:1275–1278, 1986.

Castner, S., R. Early, and B.R. Carlton. Anabolic steroid effects on body composition in normal young men. *J. Sports Med. Phys. Fitness* 11:98–103, 1971.

Celejowa, I. and M. Homa. Food intake, nitrogen and energy balance in Polish weight lifters during a training camp. *Nutrition and Metabolism* 12:259–274, 1970.

Consolazio, C.F., H.L. Johnson, R.A. Dramise, and J.A. Skata. Protein metabolism during intensive physical training in the young adult. *Am. J. Clin. Nutr.* 28:29–35, 1975.

Costill, D.L., A. Bennett, G. Brahnam, and D. Eddy. Glucose ingestion at rest and during prolonged severe exercise. *J. Appl. Physiol.* 34:764–769, 1973.

Costill, D.L., E. Coyle, G. Dalsky, W. Evans, W. Fink, and D. Hopes. Effects of elevated plasma FFA and insulin on muscle glycogen usage during exercise. *J. Appl. Physiol.* 43:695–699, 1977.

Costill, D.L., E.F. Coyle, W.F. Fink, G.R. Lesmes, and F.A. Witzmann. Adaptations in skeletal muscle following strength training. *J. Appl. Physiol.* 46:96–99, 1979.

Costill, D.L. and J.M. Miller. Nutrition for endurance sport: Carbohydrate and fluid balance. *Int. J. Sports Med.* 1:2–14, 1980.

Coyle, E.F., S. Bell, D.L. Costill, and W.J. Fink. Skeletal muscle fiber characteristics of world-class shot-putters. *Research Quarterly* 49:278–284, 1978.

Crist, D.M., P.J. Stackpole, and G.T. Peake. Effects of androgenic–anabolic steroids on neuromuscular power and body composition. *J. Appl. Physiol.* 54:366–370, 1983.

Dohm, G.L., G.J. Kasperek, E.B. Tappscott, and E.B. Beecher. Effect of exercise on synthesis and degradation of muscle protein. *Biochem. J.* 188:255–262, 1980.

Dons, B., K. Bollerup, F. Bonde–Petersen, and S. Hancke. The effect of weight-lifting exercise r elated to muscle fiber composition and muscle cross-sectional area in humans. *Eur. J. Appl. Physiol.* 40:95–106, 1979.

Dragan, G.I.A., A. Vasiliu, and E. Georgescu. Effect of increased supply of protein on elite weight–lifters. In: *Milk Proteins.* T.E. Galesloot and B.J. Tinbergen (Eds.) Wageningen, The Netherlands: Prodoc, 1985, p.99–103.

Edgerton, V.R. Mammalian muscle fiber types and their adaptability. *Amer. Zool.* 18:113–125, 1978.

Edgerton, V.R. Neuromuscular adaptation to power and endurance work. *Can. J. Appl. Sport Sci.* 1:49–58, 1976.

Fahey, T.D. (Ed.) *Athletic Training: Principles and Practice.* Mountain View, Ca.: Mayfield Publishing, 1986.

Fahey, T.D., L. Akka, and R. Rolph. Body composition and VO_2max of exceptional weight-trained athletes. *J. Appl. Physiol.* 39:559–561, 1975.

Fahey, T.D. and C.H. Brown. The effects of an anabolic steroid on the strength, body composition, and endurance of college males when accompanied by a weight training program. *Med. Sci. Sport* 5:272–276, 1973.

Fleck, S.J. and W.J. Kraemer. Resistance training: Physiological responses and adaptations. *Physician and Sports Med.* 16:108–124, 1988.

Foster, C., D.L. Costill, and W.J. Fink. Effects of pre-exercise feedings on endurance performance. *Med. Sci. Sports* 11:1–5, 1979.

Fowler, W.M., G.W. Gardner, and G.H. Egstrom. Effect of an anabolic steroid on the physical performance of young men. *J. Appl. Physiol.* 20:1038–1040, 1965.

Fox, E.L. *Sports Physiology.* Philadelphia, Pa.: W.B. Saunders Co., 1979, 242–281.

Frankle, M.A., G.J. Cicero, and J. Payne. Use of androgenic anabolic steroids by athletes. *JAMA* 252:482, 1984.

Geliebter, A., E.F. Bracco, T.B. Van Itallie, and S.A. Hashim. Medium-chain triglyceride diet and obesity. *Int. J. Obesity* 8:191–192, 1984.

Gledhill, N. Blood doping and related issues: A brief review. *Med. Sci. Sports Exercise* 14:183–189, 1982.

Goldberg, A.L. Mechanisms of growth and atrophy of skeletal muscle. In: R.G. Cassens (Ed.) *Muscle Biology.* New York, NY: Marcel Dekker, Inc., 1972.

Gollnick, P.D., K. Piehl, I.V. Saubert, C.W. Armstrong, and B. Saltin. Diet, exercise, and glycogen changes in human muscle fibers. *J. Appl. Physiol.* 33:421–425, 1972.

Gontzea, I., R. Sutzescu, and S. Dumitrache. The influence of adaptation to physical effort on nitrogen balance in man. *Nutr. Rep. Int.* 11:231–236, 1975.

Gonyea, W.J. Role of exercise in inducing increases in skeletal muscle fiber number. *J. Appl. Physiol.* 48:421–426, 1980.

Gonyea, W.J. and D. Sale. Physiology of weight lifting. *Arch. Phys. Med. Rehabil.* 63:235–237, 1982.

Harkness, R.A. and B.H. Kilshaw. Effects of large doses of anabolic steroids. *Br. J. Sports Med.* 9:70–73, 1975.

Haskell, W., J. Scala, and J. Whittam (Eds.). *Nutrition and Athletic Performance.* Palo Alto, Ca.: Bull Publishing Co., 1982.

Haupt, H.A. and G.D. Rovere. Anabolic steroids: A review of the literature. *Am. J. Sports Med.* 12:469–484, 1984.

Haymes, E.M. Nutritional concerns: Needs for iron. *Med. Sci. Sports Exerc.* 19(Suppl.):197–200, 1987.

Hickson, R.C. Interference of strength development by simultaneously training for strength and endurance. *Eur. J. Appl. Physiol.* 45:255–263, 1980.

Hickson, R.C., M.J. Rennie, W.W. Winder, and J.O. Holloszy. Effects of increased plasma fatty acids on glycogen utilization and endurance. *J. Appl. Physiol.* 43:829–833, 1977.

Hill, J.A., J.R. Suker, K. Sachs, and C. Brigham. The athletic polydrug abuse phenomenon: A case report. *Am. J. Sports Med.* 11:269–271, 1983.

Ho, K.W., R.R. Roy, C.D. Tweedle, W.W. Heusner, W.D. Van Huss, and R.E. Carrow. Skeletal muscle fiber splitting with weight-lifting exercise in rats. *Amer. J. Anat.* 157:433–440, 1980.

Holma, P. Effects of anabolic steroid (metandienone) on spermatogenesis. *Contraception* 15:151–162, 1977.

Ivy, J.L., D.L. Costill, W.J. Fink, and R.W. Lower. Influence of caffeine and carbohydrate feedings on endurance performance. *Med. Sci. Sports* 11:6–11, 1979.

Ivy, J.L., D.L. Costill, W.J. Fink, and E. Maglischo. Contribution of medium and long chain triglyceride intake to energy metabolism during prolonged exercise. *Int. J. Sports Med.* 1:15–20, 1980.

Jansson, E. Diet and muscle metabolism in man. *Acta Physiol. Scand.* (Supp.)487:1–24, 1980.

Jette, M., O. Pelletier, L. Parker, and J. Thoden. The nutritional and metabolic effects of a carbohydrate-rich diet in a glycogen supracompensation training regimen. *Am. J. Clin. Nutr.* 31:2140–2148, 1978.

Johnson, C.C., M.H. Stone, R.J. Byrd, and S.A. Lopez. The response of serum lipids and plasma androgens to weight training exercise in sedentary males. *J. Sports Med.* 23:39–44, 1983.

Johnson, L.C., G. Fisher, L.J. Sylvester, and C.C. Hofheins. Anabolic steroid: Effects on strength, body weight, oxygen uptake and spermatogenesis upon mature males. *Med. Sci. Sports* 4:43–45, 1972.

Karlsson, J. and B. Saltin. Diet, muscle glycogen, and endurance performance. *J. Appl. Physiol.* 31:203–206, 1971.

Kasperek, G.J. and R.D. Snider. Increased protein degradation after eccentric exercise. *Eur. J. Appl. Physiol.* 54:30–34, 1985.

Katch, F. and W.D. McArdle. *Nutrition, Weight Control, and Exercise.* Boston, Ma.: Houghton Mifflin Co., 1977.

Kindermann, W., J. Keul, and G. Huber. Physical exercise after induced alkalosis (bicarbonate or tris-buffer). *Europ. J. Appl. Physiol.* 37:197–204, 1977.

Kochakian, C.D. (Ed.) *Anabolic–androgenic Steroids.* Berlin, W. Germany: Springer–Verlag, 1976.

Koivisto, V.A., S.L. Kavonen, and E.A. Nikkila. Carbohydrate ingestion before exercise: Comparison of glucose, fructose, and sweat placebo. *J. Appl. Physiol.* 51:783–787, 1981.

Lamb, D.R. Anabolic steroids in athletics: How well do they work and how dangerous are they? *Amer. J. Sports Med.* 12:31–38, 1987.

Lamb, D.R. Androgens and exercise. *Med. Sci. Sports* 7:1–5, 1975.

Laritcheva, K., N. Yalovaya, P. Smirnov, V. Schubin, V. Belaev, and M. Kim. Protein needs of highly qualified weight-lifters. *Tyach. Atlet.* 32–33, 1978.

Lemon, P.W.R. Protein and exercise: Update 1987. *Med. Sci. Sports Exerc.* 19(Suppl.):179–190, 1987.

Lesmes, G.R., D. Costill, E.F. Coyle, and W.J. Fink. Muscle strength and power changes during maximal isokinetic training. *Med. Sci. Sports* 10:266–269, 1978.

MacDougall, J.D., G.R. Ward, D.G. Sale, and J.R. Sutton. Biochemical adaptation of human skeletal muscle to heavy resistance training and immobilization. *J. Appl. Physiol.* 43:700–703, 1977.

Marconi, C., G. Sassi, A. Carpinelli, and P. Ceretelli. Effects of L-carnitine loading on the aerobic and anaerobic performance of endurance athletes. *Eur. J. Appl. Physiol.* 54:131–135, 1985.

Marconi, C., G. Sassi, and P. Ceretelli. The effect of alpha-ketoglutarate-pyrodoxine complex on human maximal aerobic and anaerobic performance. *Eur. J. Appl. Physiol.* 49:307–317, 1982.

Merkin, G. Carbohydrate loading: A dangerous practice. *J. Am. Med. Assoc.* 223:1511–1512, 1973.

Meyers, F.H., E. Jawetz, and A. Goldfien. *Review of Medical Pharmacology.* Los Altos, Ca.: Lang Medical Pub., 1980.

Morgan, W. (Ed.) *Ergogenic Aids and Muscular Performance.* New York, NY: Academic Press, 1972.

Moritani, T. and H.A. deVries. Potential for gross muscle hypertrophy in older men. *J. Gerontology* 35:672–682, 1980.

National Strength Coaches Association. Periodization. *NSCA Journal* 8:12–22, 1986.

Noakes, T. *Lore of Running.* Cape Town, South Africa: Oxford University Press, 1985.

O'Shea, J.P. The effects of an anabolic steroid on dynamic strength levels of weight lifters. *Nutr. Rep. Int.* 4:363–370, 1971.

O'Shea, P. Effects of selected weight training programs on the development of strength and muscle hypertrophy. *Research Quarterly* 37:95–102, 1964.

Page, L. and E. Phippard. *Essentials of an Adequate Diet. Home Economics Research Report No. 3.* U.S. Department of Agriculture, Washington D.C., 1957.

Pate, R.R., M. Maguire, and J. Van Wyk. Dietary iron supplementation in women atheltes. *Physician and Sportsmed.* 7:81–101, 1979.

Percy, E.C. Ergogenic aids in athletics. *Med. Sci. Sports* 10:298–303, 1978.

Pernow, B. and B. Saltin (Eds.). *Muscle Metabolism During Exercise.* New York, NY: Plenum Press, 1971.

Peterson, G.E. and T.D. Fahey. HDL–C in five elite athletes using anabolic-androgenic steroids. *Physician Sportsmed.* 12(6):120–130, 1984.

Rich, V. Drugs in athletics: Mortality of Soviet athletes. *Nature* 311:402–403, 1984.

Senior, J.R. (Ed.) *Medium Chain Triglycerides.* Philadelphia, Pa.: University of Pennsylvania Press, 1968.

Sjostrom, M. and J. Friden. Muscle soreness and muscle structure. *Med. Sport Sci. Exerc.* 17:169–186, 1984.

Smith, N.J. *Food for Sport.* Palo Alto, Ca.: Bull Publishing Co., 1976.

Smith, N. Nutrition and athletic performance. *Medical Times* 109:91–107, 1981.

Stamford, B.A. and R. Moffatt. Anabolic steroid: Effectiveness as an ergogenic aid to experienced weight trainers. *J. Sports Med. Phys. Fitness* 14:191–197, 1974.

Staron, R.S., F.C. Hagerman, and R.S. Hikida. The effects of detraining on an elite power lifter. *J. Neurological Sciences* 51:247–257, 1981.

Strauss, R.H., J.E. Wright, and G.A.M. Finerman. Anabolic steroid use and health status among forty-two weight-trained male athletes. *Med. Sci. Sports* 14:119, 1982.

Strauss, R.H., J.E. Wright, G.A.M. Finerman, and D.H. Catlin. Side effects of anabolic steroids in weight-trained men. *Physician and Sports Med.* 11:87–96, 1983.

Stromme, S.B., H.D. Meen, and A. Aakvaag. Effects of an androgenic–anabolic steroid on strength development and plasma testosterone levels in normal males. *Med. Sci. Sports* 6:203–208, 1974.

Surburg, P.R. Neuromuscular facilitation techniques in sports medicine. *Physician Sportsmed.* 9:115–127, 1981.

Taylor, W.N. *Anabolic Steroids and the Athlete.* Jefferson, NC: McFarland & Co., 1982.

Tesch, P.A., P.V. Komi, and K. Hakkinen. Enzymatic adaptations consequent to long-term strength training. *Int. J. Sports Med.* 8(Suppl.):66–69, 1987.

Thorstensson, A. Muscle strength, fibre types and enzyme activities in man. *Acta Physiol. Scand.* 443(Suppl.):1–45, 1976.

Verkhoshansky, U. How to set up a training program in speed–strength events (part 1). *Legkaya Atletika* 8:8–10, 1979. Translated in: *Soviet Sports Review* 16:53–57, 1981.

Verkhoshansky, U. How to set up a training program in speed–strength events (part 2). *Legkaya Atletika* 8:8–10, 1979. Translated in: *Soviet Sports Review* 16:123–126, 1981.

Ward, P. The effect of an anabolic steroid on strength and lean body mass. *Med. Sci. Sports* 5:277–282, 1973.

Williams, M.H. *Drugs and Athletic Performance.* Springfield, Il.: Charles C. Thomas, 1974.

Williams, M.H. *Nutritional Aspects of Human Physical and Athletic Performance.* Springfield, Il.: Charles C. Thomas, 1976.

Williams, M.H. (Ed.) *Ergogenic Aids in Sport.* Champaign, Il.: Human Kinetics Publishers, 1983.

Wright, J. Anabolic steroids and athletics. *Exercise and Sports Science Reviews* 8:149–202, 1980.

Wright, J. *Anabolic Steroids and Sports.* Natick, Ma.: Sports Science Consultants, 1978.

Wright, J. *Anabolic Steroids and Sports, Vol. 2.* Natick, Ma.: Sports Science Consultants, 1982.

Index